The Students'
HISTORICAL GEOGRAPHY
OF THE HOLY LAND

BY

WILLIAM WALTER SMITH

BAKER BOOK HOUSE
Grand Rapids 6, Michigan
1954

Library of Congress Catalog Card Number: 54-11080

PHOTOLITHOPRINTED BY CUSHING - MALLOY, INC.
ANN ARBOR, MICHIGAN, UNITED STATES OF AMERICA
1954

CONTENTS

CHAPTER IX

CHAPTER X

CHAPTER XI

CHAPTER XII

PREFACE TO THE 1954 EDITION

In recent years there has been a growing need and demand for a textbook and reference book in Bible Geography. This urgent demand has come from seminaries, Bible schools and colleges, as well as from individual students of the Bible. This need is admirably met by this volume, *The Student's Historical Geography of the Holy Land,* by William Walter Smith.

This book has those specific features which are so highly valued in a textbook or reference work. It is compact, complete, scholarly, and lucid. Its wealth of information is made readily accessible through a comprehensive index. Map work, questions, and exercises at the close of the various chapters enhance the value of the book for class use.

— THE PUBLISHERS

FOREWORD

God's revelation is given to the world in three chapters. The first is the story of the land of Palestine. The second is the history of the men who made the land their home. The third is the message which the seers of Israel gave to the world.

The background of the message of the Bible is the unfolding providence of God expressed in the development of the political and religious ideas of God's people of Israel. We must know how they lived and with whom, what they did and what they thought. The background of the history is the geographical setting which made the history what it was. The story of the Hebrews is the romance of history, and Israel's place in the world has been determined in no small degree by her place on the world.

Geography and history are vitally connected. The study of the one must be interwoven with the study of the other. Geography, apart from history, is abstract and uninteresting. History, apart from geography, is meaningless. History makes geography vital because it reveals the hills and plains, the rivers and seas as the homes of men and the theatre of stirring events. Geography gives history vividness and reality. In the light of Bible geography the men of the Bible stand out as real men who lived in our world, who thought out their truth, and wrought out their destiny as all nations must.

There are two forms of geographical study which apply to religious education, physical geography and historical geography. The first gives the setting and the second the sequence of events. Purely descriptive geography study is included in historical geography. Physical geography at once determines and interprets much of the history and many of the stories of the Bible. Confined within narrow limits by the desert, the sea, and the mountains, Palestine seems to be as distinct among the lands as its people among the nations. The physical characteristics of the land are both striking and of profound significance. It lay as a narrow strip between the desert and the sea, a connecting link between the great civilizations of the Nile and the Euphrates. The strip itself is broken into zones of widely different character. Going inland from the sea, there is first a fertile coast plain, which was a highway and a battleground for all nations. Rising from the plain, along its entire length, as the Catskills rise from the Hudson River Valley, and to the same height, extends the central range. Beyond that is the deep Jordan Valley. The fall from the Judean hills to the Dead Sea is four-fifths of a mile in a distance of twenty miles. Beyond the valley the eastern plateau stretches off to the desert.

In all literalness the people of Israel were enisled among the nations. In two directions they faced the desert and the desert men. On the other sides the men and the life of all the known world lured and imperilled them. The men of Israel were at once in touch with all nations and yet, by the paradox of history, were isolated from them by their mountain homes and their natural bulwarks. The current of the world's life flowed beside them, but they were sufficiently separated to develop their own life.

The study of the physical geography will give the background and the setting for the history as nothing else will. Historical geography will locate events both in place and in time. To associate places with the events will invest the places forever with reality. To associate the events with places will show them in their relationship and sequence and will thus be an invaluable aid to the memory. The most effective method of study is by means of such expressive activities as Dr. Smith has outlined in the following pages. In relief and in color work the four zones of Palestine, with their determinating influence on the history, will be made clear. By coloring in political boundaries the pupil will learn the relation of the nations to each other, and the broad sweep of history will be made clear. By placing events in order upon a map, the details of history will be made clear.

MILTON S. LITTLEFIELD.

LIST OF MAPS IN APPENDIX

CHAPTER I

THE BIBLE WORLD

What the Bible World Includes. Speaking generally, one may say that all the principal events noted in the Bible occurred within lands bordering on the eastern portion of the Mediterranean Sea, and countries almost adjacent. The Old Testament history (Appendix) is. embraced between the four great seas of Western Asia,—the *Mediterranean,* the *Black,* the *Caspian,* and the *Persian Gulf.* The history of the life of Christ lies in *Palestine proper.* The Book of Acts and the early apostolic history includes *Palestine, Syria, Asia Minor,* and the *Roman Empire,* bordering on the Mediterranean. The Old Testament world runs from the mouth of the Nile to the Persian Gulf on the south (see maps throughout) and from Mount Sinai to Mount Ararat, near the Caspian Sea. Its total extent is about 1,400 miles east and west, and about 900 miles north and south. Its land area is about 1,110,000 square miles, or one-third that of the United States proper. Of this area, however, more than two-thirds is a vast desert, so that the occupied land amounts in extent to less than one-eighth of the United States.

Chief Physical Features of the Old Testament World. Looking at the map (Appendix) we see, in *Egypt* the *River Nile,* with its broad Delta; then traveling eastward, the *Gulf of Suez,* the *Sinai Peninsula,* containing the *Desert of Paran;* and next the *Gulf of Akabah.* In Palestine, if we cross from Joppa, we pass in order through the *Maritime Plain,* a *Central Range of Mountains,* the *Jordan River* and its wide valley, the *Eastern Range of Mountains in Gilead,* then the *Arabian Desert,* the *Euphrates River, Mesopotamia* and *Chaldea,* the *Tigris River,* the huge *Zagros Range of Mountains,* and finally the land of *Media.* (All these places should be looked up on the map and sketched in an outline map, made by the student.)

Limits and Names of Palestine. The region is rather indefinite, especially in differing times in history. The early name was *Canaan* (Num. 13 : 29), from the Canaanites, who lived there before the entrance of the Hebrews. When the ancient Hebrews took possession they called it the *Land of the Hebrews,* or the *Land of Israel.* Canaan referred to the country between the Jordan and the Mediterranean (the Great Sea) and between Mount Lebanon and the Southern Desert. Palestine is often given as a title to this section *Palestine* comes from a Greek word used to designate Philistia (Psa. 60 : 8), originally in Greek "Palaistine," and later altered by the Romans to Palestina. Philistia meant the land inhabited by the Philistines. This region of Palestine covers only 6,600 square miles, smaller than Massachusetts by some 1,200 square miles.

Palestine proper embraces both Canaan and the land east of the Jordan, often loosely termed *Gilead,* covering in all about 12,000 square miles, or equal to Massachusetts and Connecticut. Another name, given by the prophet Zechariah (Zech. 2 : 12), is *the Holy Land.* (See also Gen. 13 : 14-17 and Deut. 7 : 6.) In Hebrews 11 : 9, it is called the *Land of Promise.* (See Num. 34.) Western Palestine has about the same area as the state of New Jersey and about the shape of New Hampshire. It would extend from New York up the Hudson to within about ten miles of Albany. Palestine lay at almost the precise center of the then known world. If one were to draw a circle of 1,600 miles diameter, with Jerusalem as the focus, all the great cities of ancient times would be included,—Rome, Athens, Ephesus, Nineveh, Babylon, Memphis, Thebes, and Alexandria. It was a land shut in by mountains, which in turn shut out many enemies. Nevertheless it was the great highway between Egypt and Babylon, because, lying between both, the caravan routes passed through it with the commerce of these two mighty countries. One of the common Old Testament modes of limiting the extent of Canaan was by referring to it as "From Dan to Beersheba" (Judg. 20 : 1).

In Northern Africa (Egypt) and the Sinaitic Peninsula,
we should note the following fixed features: EGYPT lies
along the two sides of the river Nile. There have always
been two Egypts, Northern and Southern. *Northern* or *Lower
Egypt* lies in the *Nile Delta,* triangular in shape, a huge,
splendid garden, with the richest soil of the then known
world, the grain lands of the Roman Empire. *Southern* or
Upper Egypt winds along the Nile Valley, from two to ten
miles wide, with barren hills on either side, beyond which lay
desert. These two Egypts were always so separate that the
very crowns, worn by the kings, were double. The main
stream of the Nile is known as the *White Nile,* while the
Blue Nile flows into it in Nubia, rising far back in Abyssinia.
The Land of Goshen lay southeast of the Delta. It was the
home of the Israelites during their long sojourn in Egypt as
slaves. The only cities of Bible note in Egypt were *Heliopolis,*
called *On* in the Scriptures, on the eastern branch of the
Delta (Gen. 41 : 45, 50; 46 : 20), *Alexander,* in later times
the metropolis of Africa (Acts 6 : 9, 18 : 24, 27 : 6, 28 : 11);
while *Thebes* was the chief city of Upper Egypt, and its
capital.

The great SINAITIC PENINSULA lies between Egypt and the
Gulf of Suez on the one side and the arm of the Red Sea
known as the Gulf of Akaba on the other. It forms a
huge triangular desert. To the northern end lies a plain of
white sand, *the wilderness of Shur,* then below a barren
tableland of limestone, known as *the Wilderness of Paran,*
"the great and terrible wilderness" of the Forty Years' Wanderings of the Israelites (Deut. 1 : 19). It is still called
Et Tih, "the Wandering," and is crossed by two drear caravan
routes, marked by dry bones of victims to its scourge. At
its lowest point is the *Wilderness of Mount Sinai,* bordered
by *the Wilderness of Sin,* not to be confounded with the
Wilderness of Zin, lying just below the foot of the Dead
Sea. Much discussion has arisen as to the site of *Mount
Sinai,* the terms Horeb and Sinai being seemingly used in-
terchangeably. Several peaks have been claimed, presuming
that Horeb applied to the range of Mountains and Sinai to a
particular peak. *Jebel Musa,* the Mountain of Moses, is the

Mountain of the Law, according to local tradition. *Ras es Sufsafeh* has the preference of many modern writers, and, if the mountain lay at all in the south, is the most likely from its nature. The most recent critical research, favoring the shorter route of the Exodus straight across the Peninsula to the head of the Gulf of Akaba, places the Mountain of the Law near that spot.

The places of Bible interest are *Rameses* in Goshen, the starting-point of the Exodus; *Succoth* directly south a short space; *Etham* on the edge of the Lake above the Gulf; *Pi-hahiroth* and *Baal-Zephon* near the Gulf. The sites of other places mentioned as *Marah, Elim,* and *Rephidim* are altogether uncertain. (Read Exodus 12-14; Numbers 33.)

Physical Palestine in Detail. It is most important that we study the physical geography of the Holy Land in quite some detail, for, while it is true in general that geography has always left its stamp upon the history and character of mankind, it is especially true of the Hebrews, for no people of antiquity ever lived in closer contact with Nature than did they. We shall find this study of entrancing interest, for Palestinian characteristics are reflected in almost every psalm, prophecy, and parable given us in Holy Writ. "The Cedars of Lebanon, Mount Hermon, the flowing springs, the restless sea, the roaring lion, the eagle, the lily, even the sparrows" are all pictured in Bible literature. As we traverse the land, the gloomy Valley of Michmash becomes the scene of the heart-stirring attack of Jonathan upon the Philistines, that gave the Hebrews their independence from the giants. On the Plain of Megiddo, Thothmes III, Necho, and Napoleon have trodden the same paths of battle. Here is a land that Nature destined to be the great highway over which would pass and repass nations upon nations, bent on war or commerce. As we witness the location of the Hebrew homes, high on towering mountains, we can see God's plan for seclusion and education, a preparation for their contribution to the world or the world's greatest religion. And it has been the physical contour and characteristics of this land of sacred memories that has moulded the life of the dwellers among the mountains and valleys and plains that mark its face. What at first seems but a confused, unthreaded series of valleys and hills is revealed on closer inspection as an orderly, naturally-developed set of *six zones,* each with a type of life and character peculiar to its environment, each contributing directly to the special production of a distinct race and religious standard. We shall study each zone and include in each its own mountains, rivers, valleys, and cities, thus connecting them together in orderly pictorial sequence.

Questions and Manual Work on Chapter I.

1. On a world outline map (Sunday School Commission Mercator Map, Appendix) color in green crayon or water tint *Egypt,* in red *Palestine,* in indigo *Mesopotamia,* in yellow *the lands beyond the Tigris eastward,* in violet *Greece,* in black *Asia Minor,* in orange *Italy.* Put all *rivers* and *seas* in blue. Leave all the rest blank.

2. Write the names and origin of all names of Palestine.

3. Print on the map the chief physical features of the Old Testament world.

4. Copy an outline map of Palestine or a map in this book, or trace it if you cannot copy it.

5. Why is the study of Bible geography of value? How did the land determine Bible history?

JOPPA, OR JAFFA

HOUSE OF SIMON
Photo by Rev. S. U. Mitman

CAESAREA IN PALESTINE
Copyrighted by Underwood & Underwood

CAESAREA
St. Paul's Prison

Below Carmel stretches the ever-widening fertile *Plain of Sharon,* with its forests and fruitful fields, its undulating flower-beds of vernal beauty, dotted with the "Tents of Kedar." Solomon refers to "the rose of Sharon" (Song of Sol. 2 : 1). Isaiah refers to it frequently for its beauty and rich fertility (Isa. 33 : 9; 35 : 2; 65 : 10). A little farther south, it widens to twenty-five miles, and was the home for centuries of the warlike Philistines (from which the name Palestine, as we have said, was derived). In Old Testament times it was never inhabited by Hebrews. Even in Christ's time, though many Jews inhabited it, they felt like strangers in it. It was in all ages a famous war-path. Over it marched the armies of Thothmes, Rameses, Sennacherib, Cambyses, Alexander the Great, Pompey, and Napoleon. Like all coast plains, it was exposed to attack from all sides. This will account for the bravery developed in the hardy Philistine warriors. *The sea-coast* is remarkably regular, there being only one promontory or cape, where Carmel juts into the sea. There are few good harbors. We have noted Tyre and Sidon. Below are *Ptolemais, Cæsarea,* and *Joppa* (Jaffa). The See opp. p. 7 sea is shallow all along the coast. *Cæsarea* was built by See opp. p. 7 Herod in Roman times, and was of unusual beauty and wealth. S. Paul was a prisoner here for two weeks on his last voyage See opp. p. 7 to Rome. From Joppa, Jonah set sail to escape God (Jonah 1 : 3) and centuries later S. Peter had his vision of the sheet, and his call to Cornelius and the Gentile world (Acts 10 : 1-16). At *Lydda* (now Lod or Lud), S. Peter preached the See opp. p. 10 gospel. (Acts 9 : 32.) In PHILISTIA, the chief cities are *Gaza,* in the southwest corner, three miles from the sea, See opp. p. 10 mentioned from earliest times down into the book of Acts and still a city to-day (see Gen. 10 : 19; Josh. 10 : 41; 11 : 22; 13 : 3; 15 : 47; Judg. 1 : 18; 16 : 21; Acts 8 : 26). The reference in Acts is to the noteworthy baptism of the Ethiopian eunuch. *Ashkelon* was noted in Philistine times and in the days of the Crusades. *Ashdod* was the chief seat of the worship of Dagon, the fish-god. *Ekron* was the last resting-place of the Ark previous to its return. *Gath,* now unknown as to site, was the home of Goliath the giant. (1 Sam. 17 : 4, 23; 1 Sam. 5 : 10.)

The Second Zone—THE SHEPHELAH. This is the district composed of low foothills lying between the Maritime Plain and the Central Uplands. It is an open, rolling region. Here in the days of the Judges raged the intermittent warfare between the lowlanders and the highlanders. These foothills are about 500 feet only above sea-level. In the early times these combatants were Israelites and Canaanites; later, they were Israelites and Philistines; then the Maccabees fought here with the Syrians; and in the time of the Crusades Richard of England and Saladin the Saracen led the opposing armies. The *Shephelah proper* lies only between Beersheba and the Valley of Aijalon. The word means Low Country, being lower than the neighboring mountains to the East. (See 2 Chron. 28 : 18.) *The Valley of Aijalon* runs across the top of the Shephelah, just north of Jerusalem. Along this valley, Joshua pursued the Amorites, at the time when he bade the sun to stand still. (Josh. 10 : 1-14.) Through this valley, the Philistines came to attack King Saul, when Jonathan repelled them. (1 Sam. 13, 14.) *Gezer,* an important city of which King Horam was ruler, is at this valley, on the surrounding hills. (Josh. 10 : 33; 12 : 12.) Next, south from the Shephelah, lies the *Valley of the Sorek,* where Samson, born at *Zorah,* worked his wonderful deeds. Here too was *Timnath,* where Samson's first love dwelt. South of Sorek, was *Beth-Shemesh,* to which the ark was brought from Ekron, and there still spread out wheat-fields like those the lowing kine passed through. (1 Sam. 6.) A little farther south lies the *Valley of Elah,* a level plain, the battlefield where David killed the giant Goliath (1 Sam. 17). Near by is the *Cave of Adullam,* where David hid with his four hundred followers. (1 Sam. 22.) At the southern boundary of the Shephelah is the *Brook Besor,* while farther south still is the city of *Beersheba,* which marks the extreme limits of the Land of Israel. It was at different times the home of Abraham, Isaac, and Jacob. It lay on the caravan highway, and was noted for its seven great wells.

The Third Zone—THE CENTRAL PLATEAU. This is the rough, jagged, towering mountainous system, running north and south, between the Shephelah and Maritime Plain and the Valley of the Jordan River. It has three distinct divisions, each with clearly marked characteristics. They are known on New Testament maps as Galilee, Samaria, and Judea.

GALILEE is the most northern division. It is enriched by the streams that flow from Mt. Hermon, making it well-watered and very fertile. *The Leontes,* rising near ancient Baalbac, flows south through Coele-Syria (Hollow Syria) 120 miles to the sea. Numerous brooks or wadies follow in parallel lines southward, ending with the River Kishon, at Carmel's base. The name Galilee means a round object or region, i.e., well-defined and distinct. It was thus first given to a small portion or spot and then extended to include more. (Josh. 20 : 7.) At first nations not of Israelitish descent dwelt in this region. Hence it was frequently called "Galilee of the Gentiles." (Isa. 9 : 1.) The district reaches north to the Leontes, east to the Lake of Galilee and south to the Plain of Esdraelon. Upper Galilee was much higher than Lower Galilee, its mountains rising to 3,000 feet, while almost all mountains in Lower Galilee are below 2,000 feet. The mountains are in most cases broad plateaus, broken by wide, deep valleys. Of the mountains of Galilee, *Mount Tabor* See opp. p. 10 (over 1,800 feet high), on the northeast of Esdraelon, shows out clearly. (Psa. 89 : 18; Jer. 46 : 18.) Here Deborah and Barak met Sisera (Judg. 4 : 6-14). (See also River Kishon, First Zone.) *Little Hermon* (1,800 feet) is known as the *Hill of Moreh.* (Judg. 7 : 1.) It is on the Plain, southwest of the Sea of Galilee. *Endor* is on the northern slope. The witch that Saul visited lived here. (1 Sam. 28 : 7-25.) Seven or eight miles away is *Gilboa,* where Saul camped. In Old Testament times the tribes of Asher and Naphtali settled in this section. After the early settlement there is little mention of Galilee for years, until Christ's time, when a large portion of His ministry was located here. Of the cities, the following are of most importance :

Kedesh (*Kedesh-Naphtali*) was both a city of refuge and a fortified city, west of the head of *Lake Huleh* (*Lake Merom*). It was the site of the old Temple of the Sun, the ruins of which are still there, and the capital or sanctuary of the great tribe of Naphtali. It was also the home of Barak. (See Josh. 20 : 7; 21 : 32; Judg. 4 : 10; 2 Kings 15 : 29; Judg. 4 : 6; Josh. 19 : 32.) *Shunem* lies about eight miles south of Mount Tabor. It belonged to the tribe of Issachar, and is noted for the story of Elisha given in 2 Kings 4 : 8. Three miles south of Kedesh is *Hazor,* once a royal town, now a collection of broken cisterns. It is of note in the Bible. (Josh. 11 : 10; 2 Kings 15 : 29.)

See opp. p. 10 In Lower Galilee lies *Nazareth,* the home of S. Mary the Virgin and S. Joseph her husband; the place where our Lord was reared to manhood. Although shut in by hills, it was the great junction town at which converged all the many caravan routes from lower Palestine and Egypt into Asia Minor and Assyria. From the heights of the Nazareth Range near by can be seen many of the famous places in upper Palestine. The scene of more than twenty battles, most momentous in the history of the Chosen People, lay before our Master's vision as he climbed His native hills around. Here he dwelt See opp. p. 11 until thirty years of age. *Cana of Galilee* was a little north See opp. p. 11 of Nazareth and nearer to *Capernaum,* which lay on the Lake of Galilee. It was the town of Christ's first miracle (the wedding feast) and also the home of Nathanael the disciple. See opp. p. 11 (See S. John 2 : 11; 4 : 46; 2 : 1; 21 : 2.) *Nain* is on the northwest of Little Hermon. Here Christ raised the widow's son to life. (S. Luke 7 : 11.)

The highest point in Galilee is *Mt. Jebel Jermuk,* northwest of the Sea of Galilee, 4,000 feet high. A few miles west of the middle of the same Lake stands the *Kurun Hattin* or *Horns of Hattin,* a mountain 1,200 feet high, with two peaks. It is known as the *Mount of the Beatitudes,* and on its side our Lord preached his famous sermon on the Mount. Here too He fed the five thousand. (S. Matt. 5, 6, 7.) Hattin is also the historic landmark that overlooks the spot where the army of the Crusaders made its last memorable stand, and was almost utterly annihilated by the vengeful hosts of Saladin, in 1187 A. D. Esdraelon itself we shall consider as the Sixth Zone of Palestine.

LYDDA

GAZA ROAD
Photo by Williams, Brown & Earle

MT. TABOR
Plains of Esdraelon

NAZARETH

CANA OF GALILEE

SITE OF CAPERNAUM

NAIN
Photo by S. U. Mitman

BETHEL

Questions and Manual Work on Chapter II.

1. Learn to make a map of Palestine quickly. Fold a sheet of paper of the proportion of 8 x 12 inches in three divisions lengthwise. Unfold and again fold three times sideways. This gives nine squares. Draw the coast line of the Carmel Range in the upper middle square. Continue coast line to the middle of right-hand center square, lower edge. In lower right-hand corner of upper middle square place the Sea of Galilee, and at the center of its right edge Lake Huleh. Continue Jordan River southward in middle square, and place Dead Sea in upper right-hand of lower-center square. Then mark the zones on the map in colors, searching the chapters forward to find their limits. Use crayons or water colors.

2. Mark on First Zone, and print names of all cities, places, mountains, and rivers mentioned in the lesson.

3. Make a list, from west to east, and from north to south, of these same places, and write opposite each name the event in Bible history connected with it, and in a third column the Bible reference. Do not fail to look up always the Bible reference and read the passage over.

4. Do the same (as under 2 and 3) for each division of the Second and of the Third Zones.

CHAPTER III

THE THIRD ZONE OF PALESTINE.   SAMARIA

Beyond the Plain of Esdraelon, we come to the second division of this Third Zone of the Central Plateau, i.e. SAMARIA. As we pass southward we enter a land of fruitful valleys and rounded hills, covered to their tops with trees and fields, and well-watered by copious springs. The influence of this physical environment upon the inhabitants is most clearly marked. They became a pleasure-loving people, eager for ease and enjoyment, running after idols and wealth, making alliances with powerful nations that might enrich or protect them. Thus Samaria became a buffer-state, between the northern and the southern nations. Egypt and Judea on the south used it as a huge battlefield when in conflict with Syria, Assyria, Persia, etc., on the north. Samaria consequently always suffered.

See opp. p. 11 As we pass below *Bethel,* the landscape becomes more grim, the valleys narrower, more rocks appear, and stern Judea, the land of the shepherd, in contrast to Samaria, the haven of the farmer, lies before us. Judea spelt a desperate struggle, and it alone could produce men of courage and deep intensity, such as Isaiah, Amos, and the like. The real stamina of all Palestine was developed and nourished in this southern section of the wild Judean plateau. Let us traverse Samaria and Judea in detail.

See opp. p. 14 *Samaria* of the New Testament was always *Mount Ephraim* of the Old. Here Ephraim, half of Manasseh, and the tribe of Dan dwelt. Many of the greatest events of Bible history occurred within its borders. After the captivity of the Northern Kingdom of Israel it was filled by foreign peoples sent in by the Assyrians and Babylonians. At Christ's coming, "the Jews had no dealings with the Samaritans," regarding them and their land as polluted. Samaria stretched from the edge of Esdraelon on the north to below Bethel on the south, and from the Jordan to the Plain of Sharon. Although only about twenty-five miles in length, the Jews were so averse to passing through it that they usually crossed the Jordan at the Beth-shan Fords and recrossed at Jericho, in journeying from Galilee to Judea.

Samaria has an average elevation of about 2,000 feet above sea-level, being not so much a mountain mass as a series of high ridges, with plains and elevated valleys between. The slope on the west, towards the Maritime Plain, is gradual; while that on the east to the Jordan River is exceedingly steep and precipitous. In the southern part, it rises 2,800 feet in only nine miles. The chief mountains of Samaria are Mounts Carmel, Gilboa, Ebal, Gerizim and Baal-Hazor. *Mount Carmel* is a ridge rather than a single mountain, just as are Mt. Hermon and Mt. Lebanon. It runs in from the only cape or promontory of the sea-coast, below Phoenicia, with the River Kishon at its base, in a general direction midway between the foot of the Sea of Galilee and the head of the Dead Sea. It is about 12 miles long. At the southeastern end, where it slopes out into low hills, lies the rich *Valley of Dothan,* in which Joseph found his brethren tend- See opp. p. 14 ing their flocks the day they sold him as a slave. (Gen. 37 : 17.) The Carmel range is of limestone, honeycombed with long, winding caves. Carmel means "Park," and in the Hebrew it is usually "The Park." (See Isa. 35 : 2; Cant. 7 : 5; Amos 1 : 2.) The mountains became a sanctuary or holy spot, in which worship was offered both to Jehovah and to idols. (1 Kings 18 : 19.) *Mount Gilboa* is a barren peak, See opp. p. 14 1,700 feet high, running as a ridge along ten miles, edging the southern border of the Plain of Esdraelon. Here occurred the defeat and death of Saul and Jonathan. (2 Sam. 1 : 17-27.) Here too Gideon gathered his little army of the faithful three hundred. (Judg. 6-8.) *Mount Ebal and Mount Gerizim* lie about the center of Samaria, Ebal (mount of cursing) lay northward; while Gerizim (mount of blessing) lay southward, with the bases not more than a quarter of a mile apart. *The valley and city of Shechem* lay between See opp. p. 14

them. Ebal is 3,076 feet high; Gerizim is 2,848; while the valley is 1,672 feet. Into this valley, Joshua led the entire assemblage of Israelites after the crossing of the Jordan. All
came, men, women, and children. The Levites stood in the
Valley, with the tribes, half-and-half on the mountains on
either side. The Levites read the curses of the law on sin,
the tribes on Ebal replied in answer "Amen." They then
read the blessings of the law on virtue, and the tribes on
Gerizim replied "Amen." Later on, before his death, Joshua
again gathered the people here, to listen to his parting coun-
sels. (See Deut. 27; Josh. 8, 24.) Some years later, Jotham
(Judg. 9) told the men of Shechem his parable of the trees
choosing a king, speaking from a bluff near by, and then
ran away to escape their anger. In the period of the res-
toration of Jerusalem, after the exile, the Samaritans were
rejected from participation in the worship of the Temple at
Jerusalem. They then set up a temple on Mount Gerizim.
When Christ met the woman of Samaria, she spoke to Him
of that worship, saying "Our fathers worshipped in this mountain." (S. John 4 : 20.) That temple however had been destroyed 170 years before. Shechem has had many names.
Its present name is *Nablous.* It is also practically the site of
See opp. p. 15 *Sychar,* where Jacob's Well stands, and where our Lord met
the Samaritan Woman, referred to above. It has been the
common opinion that Shechem and Sychar were the same;
but much recent research seems to indicate that they were
two separate towns, Sychar being about two miles to the
southeast of Shechem. Sychar has been identified with Askar, at the base of Mount Ebal. The Samaritan name Shechem closely resembled Sychar, and the two were confounded
by the Crusaders, so that Shechem was said to be Sychar.
Explorations have made the situation of Jacob's Well one
of the most assured spots in Palestine, and located Askar
and Sychar as identical. The proximity of the two towns
however makes them practically one situation. At Shechem,
Abimelech, the usurper, set up his brief kingdom. Another
usurper, Jeroboam, the son of Nebat, was crowned here by
the Ten Tribes. (1 Kings 12 : 25.) Another name seems
to have been *Neapolis,* in the Grecian Period. In the early

REMAINS OF SAMARIA

PLAIN OF DOTHAN
Copyrighted by Underwood & Underwood

BATTLEFIELD OF GIDEON
Copyrighted by Underwood & Underwood

SHECHEM
Copyrighted by Underwood & Underwood

SYCHAR

JACOB'S WELL

JEZREEL
Photo by S. U. Mitman

RAMAH

dawn of the history of Israel, Abram, coming across the Jordan, built his first altar to God, and rested in Shechem. (Gen. 12 : 7.)   Before the exodus was completed by the conquest of Canaan, the people regarded it as holy. (Deut. 11 : 29; Josh. 24 : 32.)   Near it were *Joseph's Tomb* (Gen. 33 : 19; S. John 4 : 6) and *Jacob's Well. Baal-Hazor,* twenty See opp. p. 15 miles south of Gerizim, five miles north of Bethel, is the highest mountain of Samaria, 3,300 feet.   On its slope Absalom had his sheep-shearing farm, where at a great feast he had summoned, he treacherously killed his brother Amnon. (2 Sam. 13 : 2-29.)

Among other cities to be considered is *Jezreel,* seated on a See o. p. p. 15 foothill of Mount Gilboa.   It commanded a vista over the entire valley of Jezreel. (2 Kings 9 : 17.)   Ahab and Jezebel made it their capital, when that wicked king reigned in Israel.   His royal palace stood on the eastern wall of the city, and from its window Jezebel was cast down to the hungry dogs below, in the open space where the city refuse was thrown.   (2 Kings 9 : 30-35; 1 Kings 21 : 1.)   The vineyard of Naboth was hard by the palace.   The modern name is *Zerin,* though only a collection of ruined huts remains. *Tirzah* is another city of this region, probably near Shechem, though its site is not yet definitely fixed.   It was noted for its beauty and was, at one time, the second royal city.   Zimri was besieged there, and to avoid capture, set fire to his palace and was burned himself.   (Song of Sol. 6 : 4; 1 Kings 14 : 17; 15 : 33; 16 : 18.)   Six miles northwest of Shechem and twenty-three miles from the seacoast, lies the *Mount or Hill of Samaria,* standing isolated and alone in the midst of a wide green basin.   King Omri, the father of Ahab, bought it of Shemer, its owner, for two talents of silver.   From the name of its owner, Omri gave the town the title of Shomeron, which became altered to Samaria. From that time on it was the capital of the Northern Kingdom of Israel.   The city was almost impregnable.   It withstood two severe sieges, 901 and 910 B. C., and Shalmaneser finally took three years to capture it.   (1 Kings 20 : 1; 2 Kings 6 : 24-27 : 20; 18 : 9, 10.) · Under Ahab and Jezebel, it became the center for an ornate idolatrous worship, in its most licentious forms. (Isa. 28 : 1-4.) Near the time of Christ it was rebuilt by King Herod, and named *Sebaste,* the Greek of Augustus, equivalent to Augusta. The colonnades and pillars of Herod, all in ruins, still remain standing, as a mute witness to the city's pristine grandeur. The old name clung to it, and it was known in Christ's time as Samaria. S. Philip preached with great success in the city in its power, "there was great joy in the city." (Acts 8 : 5-8.) The ruins of the Church of St. John the Baptist, built by the Crusaders, still stand upon the slope of the hill, erected in the twelfth century. It ran more than 3,000 feet with its sweeping colonnade. The remains of an old reservoir, the *Pool of Samaria,* are also to be seen, where was once washed the blood-stained chariot of Ahab, when the infamous king met his doom. (1 Kings 22 : 38.) Well indeed has the prophecy of Micah the prophet been literally fulfilled. (Micah 1 : 1-6.)

Shiloh, now called *Seilun,* lies in a secluded valley, twelve miles southeast of Shechem, nine miles north of Bethel. Its site is definitely named in Judges 21 : 19. Its ruins have been positively identified.

For about 400 years, in the period of the Judges, Shiloh was the seat of the tabernacle worship, and the Ark of the Covenant was kept here. It was the most esteemed sanctuary of the whole land. (Josh. 18; Judg. 21 : 19.) In later years the ark was lost to Shiloh through its capture by the Philistines. (1 Sam. 4.) When the tribe of Benjamin had been all but exterminated by the other tribes, the men repaired to Shiloh and captured the young women of the town, to be their wives, and so rehabilitate the tribe. (Judg. 21 : 19-23.)

At Shiloh, Joshua completed the division of the land among the tribes. (Josh. 18 : 6.) Here Eli ministered as high priest, and Samuel grew up as a child. At Shiloh lived the prophet Ahijah, whom the wife of Jeroboam came to visit, concerning the life of her sick son. (1 Kings 14 : 2.) *Gilgal,* seven miles north of Bethel, should be distinguished from the Gilgal near Jericho, where Israel encamped after crossing the Jordan. This northern Gilgal is the place where

Samuel set up a school of the prophets, from which Elijah went to Bethel, and then on to Jericho, on his last visit to the "sons of the prophets." (2 Kings 2 : 1; 4 : 38.)

Besides the rivers flowing into the Mediterranean, which take their rise in the mountains of Ephraim or Samaria, all of which we have studied under the Maritime Plain, we have one river of Bible mention, flowing eastward into the Jordan, *the Farah.* It rises at the base of Mount Ebal. It is "the waters of Enon," mentioned by S. John. (S. John 3 : 23.)

Questions and Manual Work on Chapter III.

1. What Old Testament events are connected with the places of the Maritime Plain? the Plain of Sharon? Philistia?

2. What Old Testament events are connected with localities in the Shephelah? In Galilee?

3. What New Testament events, if any, are connected with these several divisions?

4. Draw an outline map of the region of Samaria, alone, making it on a scale at least four inches across. On it locate the places, mountains, rivers, etc., in proper order, by dot and name.

5. Make a list, as in previous chapter, of places in order of events and Bible references.

CHAPTER IV

THE THIRD ZONE OF PALESTINE. CONTINUED. JUDEA

The third great division, southward, of the Third Zone, that of the Central Plateau, is JUDEA, that portion of Canaan which in the settlement of the land was assigned by Joshua to the tribes of Benjamin, Judah, Simeon, and Dan. Judah and Benjamin were the most important, and the former, in fact, the chief ruling tribe of all. Simeon seems to have had part of the dry South Land or Negeb, next the desert. Dan was west of Benjamin, between the valleys of Aijalon and Sorek. (Josh. 15-19.) All this territory became practically the kingdom of Judah, the southern kingdom, after the division ensuing upon Solomon's death. It was called the Kingdom of Judah. After the return from exile it became Judea and its inhabitants Jews. The exceedingly mountainous character of this part of Palestine has ever made the sturdy nature of this people. Every nation and tribe that dwelt there developed hardihood and courage, high principles and noble morals. For many centuries, the inhabitants kept very much to themselves, hemmed in by rocky walls. They took no part in the wars of Gideon and Barak, and held aloof from either progress, conquest, or commerce. Yet this very isolation enabled Judea to hold out against the great world powers, Babylon, Assyria, Egypt, Rome, for a century and a half after the Northern Kingdom was extinct. The entire size of this territory was but thirty miles wide, from the Jordan to the Philistine Plain, and fifty-five miles long, from Geba to Beersheba, 1,500 square miles in all (see 2 Kings 23 : 8), less than half as large as the State of Rhode Island. Judea has always been a land of shepherds, although as a whole it is a rocky, barren, rugged land—mountains, wilderness, stones everywhere—and in the

18

southern extremity, wild, desolate, and uninviting. It is also an unusually dry section. In the whole length and breadth there are not more than six or seven streams that have water the entire year. Scanning the country in detail, from the north downwards, as we did the other sections, we would locate two towns by name, for their sites are uncertain, just below Gilgal, our last town in the Middle Section, Samaria. One of these towns is *Gophna,* probably the modern village of Jufna, the most northerly on the western plateau of Judea. It was called *Ophni* at the time of the conquest. (Josh. 18 : 24.) It was the last halting-place of Titus on his ill-fated march to Jerusalem. *Orphrah,* the second, was a frontier town on the northeast corner, thirteen miles north of Jerusalem. It has been identified with *Ephron or Ephraim,* mentioned in 2 Chron. 13 : 19 and S. John 11 : 54, where Christ rested from the throng, after the raising of Lazarus.

Bethel, "the house of God," modern *Beitin,* is on the main road, ten miles north of Jerusalem, seven south of Gilgal. The ridge of mountain on which the ruins of the ancient city still stand, is almost 2,900 feet above the sea. There are now, says Dr. Schaff, "about two dozen Moslem hovels, the ruins of a Greek church, a very large cistern, and wild rocks." Scarcely any spot in all the Holy Land has so many events gathered around it. Abraham first rested here on his journey south from Shechem. (Gen. 12 : 8.) Here Lot surveyed the land and selected his future residence. (Gen. 13 : 1-10.) Here Jacob in his flight rested on a stone and dreamed his vision of angels. (Gen. 28 : 10-22.) It was one of Samuel's sacred sanctuaries. (Judg. 20 : 18, 26-28; 21 : 4; 1 Sam. 7 : 16.) Jeroboam made it a city of idol worship. (1 Kings 12 : 27-29, 32, 33; 13 : 1-10.) Part of the time it was held by the Northern Kingdom and part by the Southern. (See Picture 15.) *Ai or Hai,* mentioned in Joshua 8, is probably the heap of ruins two miles east of Bethel. *Rock Rimmon,* a small village four miles east of Bethel on the edge of the plateau on the side of a mountain sloping down to the great ravine filled with numberless caves is the spot to which the survivors of the tribe of Benjamin fled after the battles noted in Judges 20 : 28-47. *Michmash (Mukmas)* has

been placed at the modern village four miles southeast of
Bethel. The rocky gorge up which Jonathan climbed and the
spot from which he began his perilous descent (1 Sam. 14 :
13) are both seen here. The Philistines had come to Michmash
by way of the Valley of Aijalon, while the handful of soldiers
belonging to Saul were encamped at *Gibeah,* on the other
side of the gorge. The bravery of Jonathan and his armor-
bearer saved the day for Israel. Here, too, Joshua had
fought, in aid of his allies the Gibeonites. (Josh. 10 : 1-14.)
Michmash was also on the route of the Assyrians, as they
marched south, noted in Isaiah 10 : 28. After the exile the
remnant of the tribe of Benjamin reoccupied the spot.
(Neh. 11 : 31.) *Geba* or *Jeba* was on the south side of this
same chasm, and at the time of Josiah was the frontier town
of Judah. (2 Kings 23 : 8.) It was also again inhabited
after the exile. *Ramah of Benjamin,* six miles south of
Bethel, is one of the many Ramahs (high places) of the
Old Testament, where sacrifices were offered. It is mentioned several times in the Bible, but not with any very
special event. (Look up 1 Kings 15 : 17, 22; Josh. 18 : 25;
Judg. 4 : 5.) It is not the Ramah where Samuel was born.
See opp. p. 15 (1 Sam. 1 : 1.) *Gibeah of Benjamin,* also known as Gibeah
of Saul, may be the same as Geba; but is most likely to be
the name of a general district, including Geba and Gibeon,
on the edge of the plateau. Here occurred the almost total
destruction of Benjamin. (Judg. 19 and 20.) Here also
was the lonely watch of Rizpah, the mother of the two
young men hanged here. (2 Sam. 21 : 1-14.) *Gibeon* is to
the west of Geba, on a hill about six miles from Jerusalem.
At the foot of this hill is the *Pool of Gibeon,* where the
hosts of Abner and Joab met in battle. (2 Sam. 2 : 13.)
It was the chief Hivite city that surrendered to Joshua. At
this spot was fought the great battle of the Amorite Confederacy, which decided its fate, when the Amorites were
driven headlong down the steep Beth-horon Pass. Read the
thrilling account in Joshua 10 : 10, 11. At the great Stone
of Gibeon Amasa was slain, and at the same spot, years
later, his murderer, Joab, met his punishment by death at
the hand of Benaiah, Solomon's captain. (2 Sam. 20 : 10;

1 Kings 2 : 29-34.) At Gibeon the Tabernacle was set up after Saul slew the priests; and on the brazen altar in front of the Tabernacle, Solomon offered a thousand burnt-offerings, and here this same king made the choice of wisdom, above all other rewards. (Josh. 9 : 3-15; 2 Sam. 20 : 8; 1 Kings 3 : 4.) Just south of Gibeon is *Mizpah,* but five miles northwest of Jerusalem. It is the highest point on the plateau, nearly 3,000 feet. Mizpah is identified as the Watch-Tower of Benjamin. It was the center to which the people gathered to consult regarding the rebellion of Benjamin (Judg. 20 : 1-11) ; and again to offer sacrifices (1. Sam. 7 : 5) and to elect Saul their king. (1 Sam. 10 : 17.) It was also one of the three Judgment Cities of Samuel. (1 Sam. 7 : 16.) Gedaliah was killed here with his few followers around him. (2 Kings 25 : 22-25; Jer. 41 : 1-8.) *Nob,* a priestly city, lies near by to the east, though its site is somewhat uncertain. (1 Sam. 21 : 1; 22 : 9.) Still eastward is *Anathoth,* three miles northeast of Jerusalem, a Levitical town (Josh. 21 : 18), to which Abiathar was banished (1 Kings 2 : 26), and the birthplace of Jeremiah the prophet. (Jer. 1 : 1.)

Questions and Manual Work on Chapter IV.

1. What do you consider the four chief localities and events of the First Zone of Palestine? Of the Second?

2. What are the Divisions of the Third Zone?

3. What are the chief localities of Galilee? Of Samaria?

4. What territory did the third division of the Third Zone cover?

5. What is the chief physical characteristic of this region? How did it affect the character of the inhabitants?

6. Draw on the general map the places mentioned.

7. Make a list of the events connected with them, and a column of the Bible references.

CHAPTER V

We are now approaching the great city of all Palestine; See opp. p. 24 indeed, the most sacred city of all the world, *Jerusalem,* passing out of the country assigned to Benjamin into that belonging to the tribe of Judah. We shall consider certain mountains, rivers, and cities, in direct relation to this capital of the Southern Kingdom, in order to fix them in mind more readily.

Jerusalem is situated, roughly speaking, about one-third of the way across the head of the Dead Sea, towards the Mediterranean Sea. To be exact, it is on a mountain tableland, 2,500 feet above the Great Sea and 3,800 feet above the Dead Sea, thirty miles from the former and eighteen miles from the latter. Ravines and gorges surround the city on every side, save the north. *The Valley of Jehoshaphat,* in which the River Kidron flows, is to the east, separating the town from the Mount of Olives. The western valley is the *Valley of Hinnom.* It separates Jerusalem from the *Hill of Evil Counsel,* where the plot to betray Christ was hatched, at the base of which is the *Potter's Field, Aceldama or the Field of Blood,* bought with the price of Judas' betrayal of our Lord. The lower part of the Valley of Hinnom was called *Tophet* or the Place of Fire or *Gehenna,* and was used as a place for burning the refuse of the great city above. Let us now examine more closely some of these surrounding features, before studying the city. *The Mount of Olives* is a curved ridge, 2,637 feet high, to the east of Jerusalem. It was along this route that David passed when he fled from See opp. p. 24 Absalom. (2 Sam. 15 : 23, 30.) Here, in *the Garden of Gethsemane,* on its western slope, near Jerusalem, the Agony of our Blessed Lord took place. (S. Matt. 26; S. Mark 14; S.

Luke 24; Acts 1 : 12.) Two small mountain torrents, practically not more than winter streams, flow from this western mountain region, in this locality, and empty eastward into the Dead Sea. One is the *Brook Cherith*, probably the present See opp. p. 24 Wady Kelt, near Jericho. It was by this brook that Elijah hid from Ahab, and in his solitude was fed by God's ministrations. (1 Kings 17 : 3.) The second stream, *the Kidron*, flows through the Valley of Jehoshaphat, along the eastern side of the City of Jerusalem, between it and the Mount of Olives.

Flowing southeasterly, it passes Bethlehem and runs through the crags and wilderness of Judea, ending with a dash over the rough rocks on the shore of the Dead Sea. The valley is referred to by Joel (Joel 3 : 2, 12) and is called elsewhere the King's Dale. (Gen. 14 : 17; 2 Sam. 18 : 18.) Rubbish to the depth of 70 or 80 feet has accumulated in this valley, and the original bed of the river has moved eastward as much as 70 feet, on account of the huge piles of débris that have poured down from the heights above. The Brook Kidron is mentioned often in Bible history. Over it the bridge crossed into the City of cities, and this bridge formed part of the path the Master and His Disciples trod each time they entered the Sacred City. Ezekiel's Vision pictures it, through his creative power, as a spiritual river, rising in a tiny stream from beneath the Temple and flowing, with ever-growing volume and power, until it empties as a mighty torrent into the sea below. This, of course, was imaginative; but the symbolism of divine grace, to which it was applied, is forceful. (Ezek. 47 : 1-12.) *The Wilderness of Judah*, through which this river flows, called often the *Jeshimon*, is a long, narrow district, 10 miles wide by 35 miles long, lying on the western side of the Dead Sea. It is formed of plains of barren limestone rock, which mountain streams have furrowed with deep channels. It is a barren, desolate region, until the rainy season sets in, when, for a brief period, the "desert rejoices, and blossoms as the rose." (Isa. 35 : 1.) Somewhere in this wilderness was the cave where David cut off Saul's robe (1 Sam. 24 : 1-22) and where our Lord was tempted by Satan. (S. Matt. 3 : 1 to 4 : 1.) About twelve miles from Jerusalem, along the dreary gorge of the Kidron, on high rocks on the very edge of the gorge, stands the famous *Monastery of Mar Saba*, of the Greek Church, founded in the fifth century by S. Saba. There are only about 60 monks there now, though at one time it was filled with an assemblage of unusual men. Half way down this Wilderness of Jeshimon, the sea edge of the desert, is a fertile and wonderful oasis, called *En-gedi,* half a mile square, filled with delightful fruits and vineyards, made so by being in a hollow 400 feet lower than the surrounding plain, and so nourished with abundant water. (See Song of Solomon 1 : 14.) It is called to-day *Ain Jidy.* The old Bible name was *Hazazon-tamar, or Hazazon of the Palm.* (Gen. 14 : 7; 2 Chron. 20 : 2.) Through the Pass of En-gedi, from the rugged plateau above, the hosts of Ammon and Moab climbed up from the Dead Sea and entered that plain near *Tekoa,* known as the ascent of *Ziz.* (2 Chron. 20 : 16-20.) A few miles south of En-gedi, back of the desert, about half-way between En-gedi and the lower end of the Dead Sea, stands *Masada,* which was the last refuge of the Jews after the destruction of Jerusalem by Titus (70 A. D.). It is one of the strongest natural fortresses in all the world, 1,300 feet higher than the surrounding land, and can be reached only by men in single file, climbing a narrow, step-cut rock. The Maccabees first made a fortress of this rock. Herod the Great fled there in danger.

Returning to the country immediately around Jerusalem, See opp. p. 24 we note *Bethany,* on the road to Jericho, near the Kidron, two miles from Jerusalem, on the Mount of Olives. It was and is but a small village. Here lived S. Mary and S. Martha; here Christ raised Lazarus, their brother, from the dead; and here he often sojourned with the trio; and spent the last few nights previous to the Crucifixion. (S. John 11 : 1-44: S. Matt. 21 : 17; S. Mark 11 : 12, 19.) The site of *Bethphage.* mentioned in connection with the Palm Sunday entry, is not definitely known, but is, of course, between Bethany and the Mount of Olives.

We come now to the study of *Jerusalem* itself. The city has been known by a different name in each great period of its checkered history. In the Patriarchal time, as the seat

JERUSALEM

GARDEN OF GETHSEMANE

BROOK CHERITH

BETHANY

TOWER OF DAVID
Jerusalem

LANE LEADING TO HEROD'S
PALACE

POOL OF HEZEKIAH

CHURCH OF THE HOLY
SEPULCHRE
Exterior

of Melchizedek's priestly kingdom, it was called *Salem,* pronounced Shalem. (Gen. 14 : 18; Psa. 76 : 2.) During the Jebusite period it was known as *Jebus.* (Judg. 19 : 10.) After its capture by David, the first time it was held by the Israelites, *Jerusalem,* properly *Jeru-shalaim.* It is first mentioned thus in Judges 1 : 7, 8, where it may have come by euphony from *Jebus-shalem.* It means thus "possession of peace." It was called by the prophets by the poetic name *Ariel,* "the lion of God" (Isa. 29 : 1), and in S. Matt. 4 : 5, 27 : 53, the *"Holy City."* After it was destroyed by Titus (70 A. D.) it was rebuilt by the emperor Aelius Hadrianus, A. D. 135, and named *Aelia Capitolina,* a name it held till 536 A. D., when it resumed its old name, Jerusalem. It is now named by the Arabs, *El Khuds esh-Sherif,* "the Holy City," shortened to *El Khuds.*

We would recall that the *Valley of Jehoshaphat,* through which the Kidron flows, runs around the east and southeast; the *Valley of Hinnom* (Josh. 15 : 8) around the south and southwest, joining the former valley at Siloam, which we shall study later; and the *Valley of Gihon* (1 Kings 1 : 33) completes the western side, though some place this in the lower part of the Kidron Valley. A shallow valley, *the Tyropoeon,* shaped like a new moon, runs through the city itself, dividing the lower part into two hills. The entire city is composed of four hills. Towards the southwest, between the Tyropoeon and the Valley of Hinnom, was *Mount Zion,* 2,540 feet high. It was the highest of the hills and the one on which most of the city was built in Christ's time. On it stood the old Jebusite fortress, which was at last captured by David. Zion was known as the Upper City and also as the City of David. (2 Sam. 5 : 7-9; 1 Chron. 11 : 4-7.) *The Palace of Herod,* Agrippa's Palace, and David's Tomb were all on this mountain. Most of this portion See opp. p. 25 is now the Armenian Quarter. *The Armenian Convent,* the See opp. p. 25 largest modern building in Jerusalem; the *English Church,* the *Church of St. James,* and the *Environments of the Holy Sepulchre* are all in this quarter. On the northwest hill is Acra, 2,490 feet high, known as the Lower City, the Christian Quarter. In the lower southwest corner of this quarter is

See opp. p. 25 the *Pool of Hezekiah,* a large reservoir with a capacity of nearly three million gallons. It is supposed to be the "pool and conduit" constructed by Hezekiah to bring water to the city. (2 Kings 20 : 20.) The water comes through the conduit from the Mamilla Pool, far up in the Valley of Hinnom.

See opp. p. 25 The *Church of the Holy Sepulchre* is almost in the center of this quarter, and is really a collection of several churches and chapels. It seems to be proved without much doubt that it is not the actual locality of the burial-place of our See opp. p. 28 Lord, for a great many satisfactory reasons. It could not have stood without the second great wall of the city, without a formation in the wall-line that would have been ridiculous. The tomb is unlike the hundreds of rock-hewn tombs all around that locality and does not agree with the Bible story, and the accumulation of a large number of other impossible sites fixed around it, for manifest convenience, all tend to discredit in every way this as the true spot. As this site, with this church and a former one, has been the same since the days of Constantine, it would seem that we do not know just where the real tomb was. Perhaps this is wisely so, since God has apparently intended that none of the materials of sacred story should come down to man for superstitious veneration and perhaps idolatry. *The Moslem (Mohammedan) Quarter* lies northeast, and is the largest division of the modern city. Here are located the *Governor's Palace,* the *Church of S. Anne,* the *Pool of Bethesda,* and the *Via* See opp. p. 28 *Dolorosa.* In the wall of this quarter is *S. Stephen's Gate,* through which S. Stephen is supposed to have passed on the See opp. p. 28 way to his fateful stoning. *The Pool of Bethesda* has been recently excavated, near the Church of S. Anne, with a flight of twenty-four stone steps leading down to it, and supporting arches and porches along the sides. The Crusaders built a church over the pool, and a fresco on the wall of the crypt shows an angel troubling the water, a manifest indication that they were certain of the right site. The Via Dolorosa, along which our Blessed Lord is supposed to have passed on the way to Calvary, runs from the Governor's Palace to the Church of the Holy Sepulchre, as we have it placed to-day. Under the rock surface of the northern part of this section lie the *Royal Quarries,* from which the huge stones used in the construction of Solomon's Temple were undoubtedly cut.

Questions and Manual Work on Chapter V.

1. Transfer localities noted on special map of Samaria to the general map you are making.

2. Get an outline map of Jerusalem (or copy an outline map of same)and locate carefully, with dot and name, (a) the chief places *outside* the city walls. (b) the four divisions of the city itself, and the sites mentioned in the first three of them.

3. Make a list of places and events, as in previous Chapters, with Bible reference for each.

4. If time, try to mold a relief map in sand, clay or plasticine of the city and its valleys.

CHAPTER VI

JERUSALEM, CONTINUED. FOURTH QUARTER AND SURROUNDING ROADS

The last Quarter of Jerusalem lies to the southeast, between the Tyropoeon Valley and the Kidron Valley. It is *Mount Moriah.* On the northern corner is the site of the Temple and the southern section was known as the *Hill Orphel.* It is to-day the *Jewish Quarter.* It contains several Synagogues; but has no large buildings. Its streets are dark and narrow, densely populated, with buildings close together. Over the Temple Area, originally a sharp-pointed rock rising many feet above the surrounding land, but later made level by a wall 70 feet high, filled in with stones and earth, is a raised platform of almost five acres, paved with white marble. The original rock rises through this platform fifteen feet high. Tradition says that here Abraham sought to sacrifice Isaac; later it was the *Threshing Floor of Araunah* (1 Chron. 21 : 20; 2 Sam. 24 : 18-20); and still later the site of the Holy of Holies of the Temple. On this sacred spot have stood the Temples of Solomon, 1,000 B. C.; of Nehemiah (2 Chron. 3 : 1), often known as the Temple of Zerubbabel (586 B. C.); the Temple of Herod (time of Christ); and is now occupied by the wonderful structure, the fane of the Mohammedans, the most beautiful building in Jerusalem, See opp. p. 28 the octagonal *Dome of the Rock*, often but wrongly called the Mosque of Omar. Next after Mecca it is to the Moslems the most sacred spot in all the world, and "after Cordova, the most beautiful in any land." From the great wall to the west ran a bridge spanning the Tyropoeon, one of the remains of the arches being discovered recently by Dr. Robinson, and See opp. p. 29 named after him, *Robinson's Arch. The Wailing Place of the Jews,* gigantic stones of the wall on the eastern boundary of

28

CHURCH OF THE HOLY
SEPULCHRE
Interior

ARCH OF ECCE HOMO

POOL OF BETHESDA

MOSQUE OF OMAR

WAILING PLACE OF THE JEWS
Wall of the Temple

GOLGOTHA

S. STEPHEN'S GATE

POOL OF SILOAM

the Quarter, is the place of weekly assemblage of the Hebrews, who weep over the lost glory of the Sacred City. The Place of the Crucifixion of our Lord, *Calvary,* is pretty See opp. p. 29 definitely settled in a rounded knob or hill, outside the *Damascus Gate* (the shape of a skull), north of the Mohammedan See opp. p. 29 Quarter, not far from the Grotto of Jeremiah, outside the City Wall. The water supply of Jerusalem came partly from natural springs and partly from reservoirs collecting rain water. *The Pool of Siloam* lies on the southeast of the city See opp. p. 29 in the Valley of Jehoshaphat (Kidron) near the mouth of the Tyropoeon Valley. It received intermittent supplies of water from a spring on the northeast of the city, brought down by a long underground aqueduct. *Tophet, or Gehenna,* was a name for the lower basin of the Valley of Hinnom. Here were practised the awful rites of Moloch, and, later on, it was used as a place in which to burn the offal of the great city, so that a perpetual fire and smoke arose, and its name naturally became a synonym for the Place of Punishment. (See 2 Kings 23 : 10; Isa. 30 : 33; 66 : 24; Jer. 19 : 6, etc.) The *Fountain of the Virgin* is the only spring of running water in or about Jerusalem. It issues from a hidden source, under the foot of Mt. Orphel, about 950 feet south of the city gate. It is probably the *"Fountain of Siloam,"* referred to by Josephus, the *En Rogel,* or Spring of the Fuller mentioned frequently in the Old Testament, and the source or headwaters of the Pool of Siloam. The *Village of Siloam* See opp. p. 32 is perched on a lofty cliff, across the Kidron, opposite this Fountain. It is mentioned in S. Luke 13 : 4, in connection with the fall of its tower. The Pool of Siloam at the mouth of the Valley is fed by a long underground aqueduct, recently discovered and explored, from the Fountain above noted. At En Rogel, Adonijah held his feast. (1 Kings 1 : 19.) Solomon was anointed by the Pool of Siloam (1 Kings 1 : 38-46.) The canal or rock-hewn aqueduct is 67 feet long, so that the distance is not very great from these several sites. (See also Josh. 15 : 7; 18 : 16; 2 Sam. 17 : 17.) The Fountain was probably *the Upper Gihon* and the Pool *the Lower Gihon.* (See 2 Chron. 32 : 30; Isa. 7 : 3.) The recently recovered Pool is surrounded by massive stone steps,

recalling Nehemiah 3 : 15 and the descent of the Blind Man.
(S. John 9 : 7.)   It was the Pool from which the golden
pitcher of water was brought on the last, great day of the
Feast of Tabernacles. (S. John 7 : 37.)

Having thus explored Jerusalem and its immediate environs, let us glance back at the City of cities, e'er we follow
and examine the six chief roads leading from its portals. It
was an almost impregnable city in Bible times, particularly
in the period of the Old Testament. Encircling ravines,
much deeper then than now, surrounded it on three sides.
On the east, south, and west, it was practically unassailable,
owing to the combined natural ravine-defenses and the walls
erected above them. On the north there is no natural break
between the City and the surrounding plateau. Before the
siege of Titus (A. D. 70), this quarter was protected by
three massive rows of walls, at some distance from each
other, with towers and deep moats or ditches. Each time
these walls were broken down by enemies they were rebuilt,
not always precisely in the same spot however, so that iden-
tification of the old lines to-day, for certain periods, is somewhat doubtful. Thus the Jebusites were able to hold it a long
period, and even sent a mocking defiance to David. (2 Sam.
5 : 6.)

Six roads diverge from the Sacred City in as many directions. We shall note them and follow several to important
neighboring towns. *The Northern Road* starts from the
Damascus Gate and runs straight north, through Shechem to
Damascus. All the important towns along this route have
been visited by us in our previous chapters. *The Eastern
Road* traverses the region of crags and caves of robbers
which have ever frequented its pathway since the days of
the Good Samaritan, the road leading down to Jericho, a
continuous descent from 2,700 feet above the Sea to 1,300
feet below it in a distance of but twenty miles. It is the road
See opp. p. 32 around the *Mount of Olives* to Bethany, on its slope. *The
Southern Road* follows the crest of hills to Hebron. On it
are several important sites not yet considered. Just south
of the City is the *Plain of Rephaim,* where David twice over-
came the Philistines, after the capture of Jerusalem. (2 Sam.

5 : 18-25.)   Six miles southeast of Jerusalem, on this road, is *Bethlehem,* one of the three most important cities in all the See opp p. 32 world, Jerusalem and Nazareth being the other two.   Here See opp. p. 32 lived Jesse and David, and here was born the great Son of David, Christ our Lord.   It stands on the side and summit of a steep hill, and to-day has about 8,000 inhabitants.   In a cave near this village, Jerome wrote his Vulgate translation See opp. p. 33 of the Holy Bible, the standard version of the Roman Church. The old name of the town was *Ephrath.*   About a mile from the town is shown *Rachel's tomb.*   (Gen. 48 : 7.)   Bethlehem was the home of Boaz, the site of the exquisite story of Ruth and Naomi.   (See Ruth.   Also S. Luke 2 : 4-14.)   Just a little beyond Bethlehem lies the *Valley of Elah,* in which David fought with Goliath of Gath, leader of the Philistines. (1 Sam. 17.)   Passing on through the Jeshimon, or "the Waste," the desolate region south, the Wilderness of Judea in which lay *the Mount of the Temptation,* we come to *He-* See opp. p. 33 *bron,* eighteen miles below Jerusalem, one of the most ancient towns in the world, occupied before the days of Abraham.   In the Bible, it is called the *Vale of Hebron* (Gen. 37 : 14), and the expanse north of the town is called the *Plain of Mamre.* Hebron was built seven years before the town of Tanis or Zoan in Egypt.   (Num. 13 : 22.)   Abraham dwelt here, the See opp. p. 33 Patriarchs were buried here, Isaac, Jacob, and Joseph called it their home.   (Gen. 37 : 14.)   It was a Hittite city in the time of Abraham and a stronghold later of the Anakim.   At the Conquest it went to Caleb and became a City of Refuge. See opp. p. 33 (Josh. 14 : 10-15.)   David reigned first at Hebron and here Absalom set up his rebellion.   (2 Sam. 5 : 5; 15 : 7-12.)

The Southwestern Road runs from Jerusalem down "to Gaza, which is desert."   (See map.)   (Acts 8 : 26.)   It traverses ravines and deserts and has no towns along the route.   *The Western Road* runs to Joppa on the sea-coast. Four miles or more from the Sacred City it reaches *Emmaus,* recently identified.   This is the town and this the road where the Risen Lord appeared to his two disciples as they journeyed from the Capital the evening of his Resurrection.   (S. Luke 24 : 13.)   *Kirjath-jearim,* where the Ark rested when it was brought from the Philistines at Beth-shemesh lies along this

road. (1 Sam. 6 : 21; 2 Sam. 6 : 2.) *The Northwestern Road*
emerges from the Northern Road just beyond Gibeah, and
winds down the hills to Joppa. On it are *Mizpah, Gibeon,
and Beth-horon,* all of which we have visited.

One other city only remains to be considered, *Beer-sheba,*
which marks the southern limit of the country, far south, on
the great highroad between Palestine and Egypt.

It was at various times the home of Abraham, Isaac, and
Jacob. Abraham's wells are still there. (Gen. 21 : 31.) It
was the center of patriarchal history. Here occurred most
of the events mentioned in their lives. (Look up carefully
Gen. 21 : 33; 28 : 10; 46 : 1; 22 : 3, 19; 25 : 34; 27 : 23;
Josh. 19 : 2; Judg. 20 : 1; 1 Sam. 3 : 20; 1 Sam. 8 : 2.)
Hither Elijah fled from the wrath of Jezebel. (1 Kings
19 : 3.) Later it became a seat of idolatrous worship and
was severely denounced by God's prophets. (Amos 5 : 5;
8 : 14; 2 Kings 23 : 8.) All this south country, centering
at Beer-sheba, was called *the Negeb,* meaning "dry," bordering on the Arabian Desert, a dry, parched land. The nature
of the country demanded a nomadic life. Consequently its
See opp. p. 36 inhabitants always were a roving people. *Kadesh-Barnea,*
still farther south, 48 miles from Beer-sheba, almost out of
the Negeb, has been identified recently. *Ain Qadis* or *Ain
Quadis* had been located in 1842 and then lost track of,
until the present generation. Most of the events in Numbers
13-20 (which see and read) occurred here. *Mount Hor,* where
Moses viewed the Promised Land is just above it. (See
Deut. 10 : 6 and Num. 20 : 22-28.)

Questions and Manual Work on Chapter VI.

1. Draw from memory a rough outline map of Jerusalem,
and locate the surroundings. Make the same on the sand
table.

2. Tell or write all you know of the several Temples that
have stood on the rock in the Jewish Quarter of Jerusalem.

3. With what localities is the name Siloam connected?

4. Write down the name of each road diverging from the
City and tabulate, in order, the chief places and the events
and Bible references.

SILOAM VILLAGE

MOUNT OF OLIVES

BETHLEHEM

CHURCH OF THE NATIVITY
Interior

FIELD OF THE SHEPHERDS

HEBRON

MT. OF TEMPTATION
Photo by S. U. Mitman

TOMBS OF THE KINGS

CHAPTER VII

THE FOURTH ZONE OF PALESTINE. THE JORDAN
VALLEY TO THE GHOR

The Fourth great Zone of Palestine, to the east, is the
VALLEY OF THE JORDAN RIVER, a vast depression or
rift, extending north and south, practically the entire length
of the country. The Valley itself is the largest and most
wonderful in the world, extending from the foot of the
Taurus Mountains to the Gulf of Akabah, a distance of 550
miles. There are only three other such tracts comparable to
it, one in Asia, near the Caspian Sea; one in the Sahara in
Africa; and one in southeast California.

In ancient times, the whole of Palestine was undoubtedly
under the ocean. Then came the upheavals, causing mountains on either side, with a fall or fracture forming the
gigantic valley. At the Dead Sea it reaches a depression
of 1,300 feet, the lowest valley in the world. Professor George
Adam Smith well says: "there may be something on the
surface of another planet to match the Jordan Valley,—
there is nothing on this."

Let us study this unique region more closely. The name
Jordan means "the Descender" or "the Down-comer," be-
cause of the rushing descent of the river. *The Jordan* has See opp. p. 36
three (some say four) sources, small streams far up north in
the Hermon Range that unite to form the Upper Jordan.
The longest of these streams, forty miles long, rises 1,700
feet above the sea level, in the *Fountain of Hasbany,* at the
base of a cliff near the village of *Hasbeiya* on the western side
of Mount Hermon. The largest branch is the *Leddan,* rising
at the site of the ancient city of *Dan,* in a clear, deep pool,
the largest single fountain in the world, and from it an im-
mense body of water rushes down the valley, though the

elevation of the fountain is not more than 500 feet above the
Sea. Dan was the old *Laish,* and was conquered by the
Danites. (Judges 18.) After the Conquest, the Danites set
up a heretical worship and a graven image for idol service.
(Judg. 18 : 29-31.) Later, at Dan, the worship of the golden
calf was instituted, and it ever thereafter remained a heathen
temple. (1 Kings 12 : 28, 29; Amos 8 : 14.) The third,
and most beautiful, source of the Jordan is at the *Fountain
of Banias,* a stream issuing here, midway in size between
the Leddan and the Hasbany. This source is on the southern base of Mount Hermon. Banias is the equivalent of the
Greek name *Paneas,* the shrine of the god Pan, sacred to the
worship of Baal, the weird god of the Phoenicians, long before the Greeks adapted the grotto to the Pan-god worship,
the shepherd-god. When Rome followed Greece as Master,
Herod the Great built here a temple of exquisite white marble,
in honor of his patron the Emperor Augustus Cæsar. Philip
the Tetrarch, Herod's son, beautified the city and called it
Cæsarea, distinguishing it from the other Cæsarea on the
See opp. p. 36 coast, as *Cæsarea Philippi.* In time, the name Paneas was
restored to it, and the Arabs call it Banias. It marked the
northern limit of our Lord's travels and ministry. Near by
is *Mt. Hermon,* probably the Mount of the Transfiguration.
(S. Matt. 16 : 13-20; 17 : 1-8.) The main source recognized
by the Jews is the one at Banias. From the highest source,
at Hasbeiya down through the Dead Sea, the river is divided
into three sections, three stages or levels, each of which contains a noted lake or sea. The river passes through two of
these lakes and discharges all of its waters into the third.
The most northern and smallest lake in the first basin is
Lake Huleh, known as the *Waters of Merom* in the days of
Joshua, a triangular sheet of water three miles across, situated in an enormous swamp of dense and huge canes and
papyrus, about level with the Mediterranean Sea, never more
than 7 feet above. The second and next largest, the *Lake
of Galilee* called *Lake Chinnereth* in the Old Testament, and
the *Lake of Tiberias* in Christ's time, is a pear-shaped lake,
14 miles long by 9 miles wide, 682 feet below the sea level,
in the section we have studied as Galilee or the Esdraelon

See opp. p. 36

region. The third basin, far south, *the Dead Sea,* the largest
of all, is 46 miles long, with its *surface* 1,290 feet *below* the
Mediterranean, and in some places 1,300 feet deeper still.
Note carefully again, the downward flow of this remarkable
river. At the Hasbeiya Springs, it rises 1,700 feet above the
Sea, Mts. Hermon and Lebanon on either side. At Lake
Merom it is on a level with the Sea. Below Merom, it de-
scends with a fearful drop of 60 feet to the mile, until at
the Sea of Galilee it is 682 feet below the Mediterranean.
Here begins the gorge 65 miles long to the Dead Sea. It
flows so rapidly through the Sea of Galilee that it scarcely
mingles the waters. Along the gorge below it drops 610
feet farther in depth. It flows through the *Plain of Jericho*
on the way, which at this point is a valley 14 miles wide and
400 feet above the level of the Dead Sea, the mountains
around rising to the height of over 3,000 feet. The distance
from Hasbeiya to Lake Merom is about 40 miles, from the
entrance of Merom to the Sea of Galilee about 15 miles,
from the northern end of that Lake to the Dead Sea 79 miles,
making a direct descent in length of 134 miles. During this
descent, it falls over 3,000 feet, an average fall of 22 feet
to the mile. It varies from 80 to 180 feet in width and from
5 to 12 feet in depth.

We will now explore each of these three great basins.
Lake Huleh or *Merom* occupies the lower portion of the
Huleh basin, 12 miles below the site of Dan. At the upper
end of the basin is the huge marsh, of which we spoke, an
area practically impassable, through its reeds and papyrus,
even for a canoe. West of the lake is a rich farming region,
extending to the foot of the mountains. On this plain, by
the *Waters of Merom,* Joshua fought his victorious battle
with the Confederate Kings of the North. (Josh. 11 : 5-8.)
Yet, owing to its malaria and its insecurity from attack, it is
a forsaken, desolate, uninhabited area, not a single permanent
dwelling being found save at the border town of Banias.
From Lake Huleh, it is 11 miles in a straight line to the Lake
of Tiberias. About two miles below the upper lake the
river is spanned by a very ancient bridge, with a ruined khan
at one end, a ford of the Jordan for centuries, and probably

the identical spot that Saul the persecutor crossed on his way from Galilee to Damascus, to imprison the Lord's disciples. The Jordan on leaving Huleh Lake is 60 feet wide and 15 deep, flowing rapidly through a narrow gorge. *The Sea of Galilee* is also called the lake of Tiberias (S. John 6 : 1), the Sea of Chinnereth (Josh. 12 : 3), and the Lake of Gennesaret. (S. Luke 5 : 1.) Its length and breadth we have given. Its depth of water is about 200 feet. On its eastern side, the banks rise 1,000 feet or more. On the west, the Galilean hills descend in terraces, ending in moderate cliffs, with generally a broad belt of lowland between the cliff and the water. On the north, this gradual slope forms the fertile *Plain of Gennesaret*. The entire region is volcanic, and lava and pumice stone lie scattered about everywhere. There are but few trees, and a deserted aspect belongs to it. This Lake is little mentioned in the Old Testament; but is full of incidents of Christ's Life in the New Testament record. In the days of the Romans Gennesaret was a garden spot, all the tiny streams flowing through its plain being utilized, and for ten months each year its orchards and vineyards and fields yielded luxuriant harvests. In our Saviour's day, numerous towns and villages were nestled on its hillsides and lowlands on the western side, and every foot of land was cultivated. On the eastern side, neglect and barrenness prevailed, the desert places, to which our Lord so often retired for rest. (See S. Mark 4 : 35, 36; 5 : 21; S. Matt. 14 : 13-15.)

Only two of the many towns of this wonderful Lake, as mentioned by the Evangelists, are now inhabited, *Tiberias* and *Magdala;* and both of these are sadly changed since the See opp. p. 37 glorious days of Rome. We will commence with *Tiberias,* on the western shore about half-way towards the southern end. The city was built by Herod Antipas, and named by him for Tiberius the Emperor. Recent research shows that the enclosing wall was almost three miles long. Huge and splendid buildings were within, a citadel, theaters, amphitheaters, forum, temples, synagogues, baths, dwellings, a noble scene from across the Lake. There is no direct mention of Christ's work there; though he most certainly must have visited it. Near by were noted hot springs, which rendered

KADESH BARNEA

JORDAN RIVER

CAESAREA PHILIPPI
Photo by Williams, Brown & Earle

DEAD SEA

TIBERIAS

MAGDALA
Photo by W. H. Rau

BETHSAIDA OF GALILEE
Photo by S. U. Mitman

BROOK JABBOK
Copyrighted by Underwood & Underwood

the place particularly attractive to the Romans. Its present
population is about 5,000. *Magdala* comes next, as we go up
the west shore of the Lake. It is the modern village of
Mejdel (*Migdol* or watch-tower) at the lower end of the See opp. p. 37
Plain of Gennesaret. It was the home of S. Mary of Magdala,
the devoted friend of the Master, known in briefer form to-
day as the Magdalene. (S. John 20 : 16-18.) The town is also
mentioned in S. Matthew 15 : 39, which look up. *Capernaum,*
next north, is uncertain as to site (see cut 13) ; but the
most likely one is at the northern end of the Plain. The
city undoubtedly stood on a great thoroughfare, roads from
it leading in all directions. Of the two sites, one about five
miles from the mouth of the Jordan and the other about two,
most arguments from the records seem to favor the former.
Capernaum was an important Biblical city. It was the home
of Jesus after his rejection at Nazareth; it was in fact
called "his own city." (S. Matt. 9 : 1.)

Many of our Lord's miracles occurred here, as the healing
of the nobleman's son, healing of the demoniac, healing of
S. Peter's mother-in-law, first draught of fishes, healing of
the paralytic, healing of the Centurion's servant, healing of
the blind and dumb demoniacs, raising of Jairus' daughter,
healing of a woman with an issue of blood, of the dumb
demoniac, and of two blind men, the tribute money in the
fish, etc. Here also He called Levi or Matthew the Publican.
Two at least of His Apostles, S. Peter and S. Matthew, had
homes here, and after the rejection at Nazareth His mother,
S. Mary, transferred her own home here. (See S. Mark
1 : 29; 2 : 14, 15; S. Matt. 12 : 46; S. John 2 : 12. Also S.
Matt. 8 : 14-17; S. Mark 1 : 21-34; S. Luke 4 : 33-41.) The
town of *Bethsaida of Galilee* is just above Capernaum. Note
also the other *Bethsaida Julias,* which lies a little east and See opp. p. 37
north, up the Jordan. The former Bethsaida certainly lay
near Capernaum (S. Mark 6 : 45; S. John 6 : 17), with a
jutting headland between them. Some ruined buildings and
an octagonal fountain mark the probable site. This town was
the birthplace of S. Peter, S. Andrew, and S. Philip. Above
this Bethsaida may have been *Chorazin,* but its site is really
unknown. (See S. Matt. 11 : 21.) *Bethsaida Julias* was

originally a small fishing town. Later it was enlarged by
Philip the Tetrarch and given to his daughter, Julias, hence
its name. On a slope near by, our Lord fed the Five Thousand. (S. Luke 9 : 10-17.) On a mountain adjacent He was
praying alone when the storm broke over the disciples, on
their way across the Lake to Bethsaida of Galilee. (S. Mark
6 : 45, 46; S. John 6 : 15-17.) *Gergesa* may have been where
the ruins of a town called *Gersa, or Khersa* on the eastern
shore of the Lake, have recently been discovered. It may
have given its name to the surrounding country. . (S. Matt.
8 : 28.) The healing of the demoniacs occurred here and
the destruction of the herd of swine. (S. Luke 8 : 26; S.
Matt. 8 : 28-34.) The modern railroad to Damascus runs
up the Lake to Gersa, and thence turns eastward.

The Lake of Galilee is noted to-day for its sudden and
violent storms. On it was the stilling of the tempest. On it
S. Peter walked to Jesus. It was renowned the world over for
its variety and unusual abundance of fish, and the two
miraculous draughts of fishes came from its bosom. To-day,
not more than fifteen or sixteen small boats ply the entire
Lake, and they may often be seen all together, tied up at
Capernaum.

Questions and Manual Work on Chapter VII.

1. Write down fifteen chief localities and events of the
Third Zone of Palestine, the great mountainous backbone or
ridge.

2. Tell all you can, in description, of Jerusalem and its
environs.

3. Make a new outline map of Palestine, and draw in the
full Jordan Valley and River System.

4. Take an outline map of Esdraelon and Sea of Galilee
(or make an outline map of this region)   and place each
city and special locality (mountain, etc.), in the Galilee region,
studied thus far.

5. Make a list of these cities and the events and Bible
references.

CHAPTER VIII

THE REMAINDER OF THE JORDAN VALLEY

The Fourth Zone of Palestine.

The natives call the *Valley of the Jordan,* lying between the Lake and the Dead Sea, *the Ghor,* that is the gorge or rift, 65 miles long. On both sides the highlands rise up from 2,000 to 3,000 feet. The winds sweep across the top of these mountains, making the Ghor itself of the utmost tropical climate, a veritable hotbed. Two rivers flow into the Jordan on its way south, both coming from the east. They are *the Yarmuk* or *Jarmuk* or *Hieromax,* entering four miles from the foot of the Lake; and *the Jabbok* which comes in about See opp. p. 37 twenty miles above the Dead Sea. Within the Ghor lies an inner, smaller, and deeper valley, known as *the Zor.* At the north, it is but 20 feet below in depth; but at the south it is fully 200 feet deeper. Its width varies from one-fourth of a mile to two miles. It is jungle of tropical growth, and filled, even now, with wild animals,—wolves, leopards, and formerly lions being among them. Still again, within the Zor, at a lower level, runs the tortuous, dashing Jordan, from 100 to 200 feet wide usually; but in the rainy season a veritable flood, covering the entire Zor ofttimes. (See Jer. 12 : 5; 49 : 19; 50 : 44; Zech. 11 : 3; Josh. 3 : 15; 1 Chron. 12 : 15.)

The *Fords of the Jordan* are numerous. The river is from three to ten feet deep, and in ancient times there was not a bridge the whole way down. The Hebrew language did not possess a word for bridge. There were few towns along this Jordan Valley, partly on account of the river and partly from the prevailing malaria, the danger of invasion from wild beasts and hostile robber tribes from the eastern side of the river. On the western side, we have

Beth-shan, at the foot of the *Valley of Jezreel,* on the brow of the hill as it drops. It was held by Canaanites, though allotted to Manasseh. (Judg. 1 : 27.) Ten miles south of Beth-shan was *Abel Meholah,* the Meadow of the Dance, whence the Midianites fled (Judg. 7 : 22) and where Elisha lived, before he became a prophet. (1 Kings 19 : 15-18.)

The *city of Adam* was probably near the mouth of the Jabbok, on the east side of the Valley. (See especially, Josh. 3 : 16.) *Zaretan,* which has not been placed, was near this same river, and the district of Zaretan we know extended all along that region. *Succoth,* the place of booths, has been fixed as about a mile north of the *Damieh Ford,* which lies just below the junction of the Jabbok and the Jordan. Here Jacob dwelt for a time and built booths for his cattle. (Gen. 33 : 16, 17.) Solomon's brass foundries were also near this place. (1 Kings 7 : 46.) *Jericho,* a very important city, was situated on the western side of the Valley, here a great broad plain, about six miles from the Jordan, a mile and a half above the modern town of that name. It was the first city captured by the Israelites in the actual conquest of the land, after the wanderings in the wilderness following the Exodus. (Read Joshua 2.) Its beautiful groves of palms gave it the name *City of Palm Trees.* (Deut. 34 : 3.) It was a very wealthy city at the Conquest. (Josh. 6 : 19; 7 : 2.) The city walls then fell under providential interposition, though God, here, as elsewhere, may have used natural means, for since walls were not built strongly in those ancient days, it may well have been that the steady rhythmic stamp of many marching feet may have set up vibrations that rendered the wall quite ready to topple over when the mighty shout went up. In Christ's time the new Jericho, built below, was a noted and famous city, beautified by Herod the Great with wonderful palaces and architectural splendors. Here too the great king died. In the old Jericho, Rahab lived. (Josh. 2; 6 : 22-25.) On its fall, the curse was proclaimed against any one ever rebuilding its walls. (Josh. 6 : 26.) In the time of Ahab, Hiel of Bethel tried to revive it, and fell under the curse. (1 Kings 16 : 30-34.) One of the Schools of the Prophets was situated at

See opp. p. 52

(See opp. p. 52

Jericho, a school which both Elijah and Elisha visited. (2 Kings 2.) It should be carefully noted that there have really been three Jerichos. We have mentioned the original one and also the Roman one, farther south. The modern one, probably not older than the twelfth century, was in between the two, as we have said not two miles from the original city. It is a small Arab village of rough houses. Very recently a hotel and a Russian Hospice have been erected there. *Gilgal,* the first camping spot of the Israelites after crossing Jordan, lay a little south and east of the ancient Jericho on the Plain. Here the twelve stones of the river bed were set up for a memorial, after the passage of the stream. (Josh. 4 : 19.) Here the rite of circumcision was renewed. (Josh. 5 : 2.)

At Gilgal, the Passover was celebrated and the manna ceased when the march reached this city. (Josh. 5 : 12.) Gilgal was also the resting-place of the ark until it was removed to Shiloh. Somewhere on the Plain on its western side, probably in the south, near the northern end of the Sea, stood the *Cities of the Plain, Sodom, Gomorrah, Admah, Zoar, and Zeboim,* which were overwhelmed with destruction in the time of Abraham. It may even be the site once held by these fated cities that is now beneath a portion of the Dead Sea, for the Sea undoubtedly occupied a larger area in ancient times. The Bible descriptions of their destruction (Gen. 19; Deut. 29 : 23; Isa. 1 : 9; 3 : 9; 13 : 19; Jer. 23 : 14; 49 : 18; 50 : 40; Lam. 4 : 6; Ezek. 16 : 46, 53; Amos 4 : 11) seem to indicate a bitumen or petroleum or pitch eruption, similar to such as have occurred in the oil regions of America, due to compressed gases, intermingled with oil and water, forming flaming fire coming down from above, with cinders, smoke, ejected water, which last would supply the encrustations that may have formed the pillar of salt out of Lot's ill-fated wife. It is a remarkable proof of the influence of climate, country, and environment, that, as Professor Kent has pointed out, every race and tribe that came in and settled on this low, miasmic, tropical Plain of the Jordan Valley became in time corrupt and degenerate, morally, physically, and even mentally; whereas those in the mountainous regions, whether native or moving up from the Valley, were hardy, sturdy, high-minded, intellectual, moral for the most part, and a better race of men. Environment does mold character to a most important degree. Nearly opposite Jericho, across the Jordan, on the eastern side of the Valley, lay *the Plains of Moab, the Plain of Abel Shittim,* the meadow of the Acacias, extending from this point nearly down to the head of the Dead Sea, about fifteen miles by eight. It is still dotted with ancient, gnarled acacias, descendants of the Shittah trees of the days of Moses. (Num. 22 : 1; Josh. 3 : 1; Num. 33 : 49.) In later days, although assigned to Reuben and Gad, and specked with their fortified cities, the only remains of which to-day are heaps of earth or tells, it fell under the Amorites and became their land. Of the several Fords of the Jordan, the one of importance is *Damieh Ford,* just below the junction of the Jabbok, the crossing-place from Mount Gilead to Shechem, where Jacob crossed on his return from Padan Aram, and where the Ephraimites who could not pronounce "Shibboleth" were discovered and killed. (Gen. 12 : 6; 33 : 18; Judg. 12 : 5, 6.) *The Nimrim Ford* is opposite Jericho, often known as *the Upper Ford,* the main thoroughfare to the opposite shore. Over this ford the ark was borne at the Conquest (Josh. 3, 15, 16); here Elijah and Elisha parted the waters; and here, probably, our Lord was baptized. (S. John 1 : 28.) *The Lower Ford,* known as the *Pilgrims' Bathing Place,* is five miles below, and was used as the fords towards Moab. Ehud, Ruth and Naomi all crossed it. (Judg. 3 : 28; Ruth 1.)

The Dead Sea, of which we have spoken, is mentioned in the Bible as *the Salt Sea,* the *Sea of the Plain,* the *Sea of Arabah.* (See Josh. 3 : 16; Deut. 4 : 49; 2 Kings 14 : 25.) Its shore is desolate, lined with rock-salt and cakes of pitch, save the southeastern corner, which is fertile through fresh springs. Here at this eastern side too is the distinguishing promontory or peninsula of *El Lisan* (the tongue), 12 miles long and 6 wide. The Sea is more than five times as salty as the ocean, and extremely bitter to taste.

Questions and Manual Work on Chapter VIII.

1. Make a sand table map of Palestine, in fullest detail, at least 3 x 4 feet. Let it be carefully worked out, spending the whole hour (or more) on it. Mark cities by pin-flags ; the mountains by pole men, etc.

2. Let the class members quiz each other on the events located at the various cities, battlefields, etc.

3. Locate in detail and discuss the cities of the Jordan Valley below the Sea of Galilee.

CHAPTER IX

THE FIFTH ZONE OF PALESTINE. THE EASTERN
TABLE LAND

Climbing up the hills of Moab and Gilead, we are in **the Fifth Zone of Palestine,** in the midst of rolling, grass-covered hills, cut by rifting ravines, with dashing mountain torrents. This zone is almost entirely a highland country, its general elevation being 2,000 feet above the Sea. The backbone of the mountains is the *Anti-Lebanon range,* lower and more irregular than the Lebanon range. It is mostly a series of broken, parallel ridges. Beginning far in the north, a little above Damascus, we see a marked depression or break, separating the East Mountain of the Anti-Lebanon Range from Mount Hermon. This depression has formed the natural caravan route from Beirut to Damascus. The southern end of this upper range is broken by the deep valley of the See opp. p. 52 *river Abana, the Barada* of modern times. (2 Kings 5 : 12.) In a bend in the Abana river is the old site of *Abila,* the capital of Abilene, mentioned by S. Luke, in connection with See opp. p. 52 the Tetrarchy of Lysanias. (S. Luke 3 : 1.) *Damascus* is situated on a fertile plain, at the foot of Mount Hermon. It is watered by the beautiful Abana, which divides into many small streams, watering thus the Plain. Its surplus waters gather and are lost in a Lake at the edge of the Plain, on the borders of the desert. Probably no city of present-day existence can trace its history so far back as can Damascus. In the Bible it is often called Syria. Routes of travel lay through it in all directions. Hundreds of canals and rivulets murmur through the City and the Plain, making 150 square miles of delightful green, in the midst of which is the white, compact City and picturesque minarets. *The Awaj River,* supposed to be *the Pharpar,* rises on the sides of

Mount Hermon and flows across the Plain, a few miles below the Abana, entering another lake, below the twin marsh lakes of the Abana. (See 2 Kings 5 : 12.) The present population of Damascus is not less than 250,000. Abram visited Damascus, and his chief servant, Eliezer, came from that town. (Gen. 15 : 2.) Its first mention in the Bible is in connection with the pursuit of Chedorlaomer. (Gen. 14 : 15.) David set a garrison there (2 Sam. 8 : 6) and it became part of Solomon's Kingdom. (1 Chron. 18 : 6.) Hazael came from Damascus. (2 Kings 8.) It became the capital of Syria in the days of that pushing Kingdom. Hither Saul was journeying, to seize and imprison Christians, when he was vouchsafed a vision from God and Jesus Christ was manifested to him. Here he was baptized and restored to normal sight. (Acts 9 : 1-26.) He revisited the City later and preached boldly in the name of Christ. (Gal. 1 : 17.) From See opp. p. 53 that city he escaped in a basket. (Acts 9 : 24, 25.) Look up the many references to Damascus, noting its power and prestige, and its important place in the history of the Israelites. (2 Sam. 8 : 3; 10 : 6; 1 Kings 4 : 21; 11 : 23; 15 : 18, 19; 20 : 1-34; 22 : 1-40; 2 Kings 6 : 24; 7; 8 : 28; 10 : 32; 12 : 17; 13 : 25; 14 : 28; 15 : 37; 16 : 5.) Its final overthrow is noted in Amos 1 : 5.

EASTERN PALESTINE, as we journey southward, has three main divisions, Bashan, Gilead, and Moab. BASHAN extends from the base of Mount Hermon and the Pharpar river to the Jarmuk or Hieromax river. This division is again divided into sections. The northern section is *the district of Jedur,* the *Iturea* of S. Luke. (S. Luke 3 : 1.) It extended probably to the northern end of Lake Huleh. The Hagarites or Ishmaelites dwelt there. The name Jedur was derived from Jetur, a son of Ishmael. (Gen. 25 : 15.) The divisions of Bashan south of the Jedur are longitudinal. Next to the Jordan side, from Jedur's lower limit to the Jarmuk, was *the Jaulan,* named so from Golan, its chief city, a City of Refuge under Moses. (Deut. 4 : 43; Josh. 20 : 8; 21 : 27.) *The Kingdom of Geshur* was in this district. One of David's wives was a daughter of the king of Geshur, and her son, Absalom, fled to this region. (Deut. 3 : 14; Josh.

13 : 13; 2 Sam. 15 : 8; 1 Chron. 2 : 23.) Roman Gaulanitis must have been about equal to the same region. *The Hauran district* comes next, a level, treeless plain 50 miles long and 15 or 20 miles wide, of loose, volcanic soil, very fertile and well-tilled. The Hauran Plain is bordered on the east, between it and the desert, by *the Lejah or "Refuge"* of the Arabs, the rough region called therefore *Trachonitis* by the Greeks. (S. Luke 3 : 1.) It was also known as *Argob,* the "stony," by the Hebrews. (Deut. 3 : 4.) It is a vast mass of congealed lava, 350 square miles, or 60 miles in circumference, a black, motionless sea, with waves of petrified lava, dotted with the remains of ancient towns, for it was the stronghold of *the Kingdom of Og.* (See especially Deut. 3 : 4, 5; 3 : 14; 1 Kings 4 : 13. Recall also the reference in Psalms. Psa. 135 : 11; 136 : 20.) *Edrei* on the southern border of the Lejah was the capital, and the battlefield where Og lost his life. (Deut. 3 : 1; Num. 21 : 33; Josh. 12 : 4; 13 : 12.) *Kenath or Nobah* was also in the southeastern extremity. (Look up Num. 22 : 42; 1 Chron. 2 : 23; Num. 32 : 42; Judg. 8 : 4-11.) Some sixty other cities, "the giant cities of Bashan," were scattered over this Plain. Their ruins are still there, intermingled with magnificent remains of Greek and Roman architecture, and inscriptions dedicated to the many Christian martyrs of Decian and Diocletian Persecutions. *Job's country, the Land of Uz,* was in Southern Bashan, if we may trust traditions of the Arabs. The weight of present-day authority places Uz on the border of the desert near Petra, in the land of Edom. The extent of Bashan is about 130 miles, north and south, and from Jordan Valley to the desert. The Land of Gilead extends sixty miles from the Jarmuk to the head of the Dead Sea, at the Heshbon river. (Josh. 22 : 9.) *The Jarmuk or Hieromax* is nearly the size of the Jordan, where it enters that river. *The Brook Jabbok* cuts across a little below half way down Gilead. The part above is Northern Gilead, that below is Southern, and belonged at the Conquest to Sihon, King of the Amorites. (Num. 21 : 24-26; Josh. 13 : 25; Judg. 11 : 21, 22; Psa. 136 : 19.) Gilead is more elevated than Bashan; there is less of volcanic deposit and more of limestone; many forests of

noble trees, among them the *Wood of Ephraim,* that spelled the Waterloo of Absalom. (2 Sam. 18 : 6-14.) "The Balm of Gilead" has been sought for among these forest trees but thus far has not been discovered. Gilead was the country of Jeptha, the Judge of Manasseh, and of Elijah. The southern portion was *the Kingdom of the Ammonites.* That portion, together with the upper part of Moab, i.e. from the Jabbok to the Arnon, was *the Perea* of the New Testament, where one part of our Lord's Ministry was fulfilled and along the border of which he was baptized. (See S. Matt. 19 : 1, 13; S. Mark 10 : 1; S. Luke 13 : 22; S. John 10 : 40.) *Mount Pisgah,* (*Jebel Osha*) is the highest mountain peak, the most sightly place in all Palestine, save Mount Hermon. It is an isolated peak on the southern side of the Jabbok, "over against Jericho." From this point of vantage Moses viewed the Promised Land. (Deut. 34 : 1.) From these heights Balaam viewed the Camp of the Israelites. (Num. 24 : 5-9.) Some of the important cities of Gilead are now studied. *Gadara* is *the Um-Keis* of to-day, three miles south of the Jarmuk, and five miles east of Jordan. It was in the country of the Gadarenes, the site of the healing of the demoniacs. (S. Matt. 8 : 28; S. Mark 5 : 1; S. Luke 8 : 26.) The ruins of *Gadara* are over two miles in circumference. The site of *Mahanaim* is unsettled. All Bible references seem to indicate it as located north of the Jabbok in the land assigned to Gad, near the border of Manasseh. (Gen. 32 : 2; Josh. 13 : 30; 21 : 38.) At this spot, Jacob met the angels of God. Here Ishbosheth was crowned and later slain. Here David fled from the pursuit of Absalom. Here, in the gate, he waited for the news of the battle fought, and in the chamber over the gate he wept sore for his rebellious son. (See 2 Sam. 2 : 8; 4 : 5; 17 : 24; 18 : 24-33.)

Jabesh-Gilead is identified as probably straight across country from Dothan, at the modern Ed-Deir. It is important for connection with the following events: the defection of Benjamin (Judg. 21 : 8-14); the route of the hosts of Ammon (1 Sam. 11 : 1-11); and the rescue of the bodies of Saul and Jonathan. (1 Sam. 31 : 11, 12; 2 Sam. 2 : 5.) *Pella* is six miles northwest of Jabesh-Gilead. It is the city to

which the Christians of Jerusalem fled just before the siege
of Titus. *Peniel or Penuel* was on the Brook Jabbok; but
exactly where is uncertain. Here Jacob wrestled with the
angel. (Gen. 32.) *Gerasa* was a city of note, about twenty
miles east of the Jordan, on one of the northern branches of
the Jabbok. It was also called Jerash. It is considered the
most perfect Roman city existing above ground to-day, for
more than 200 magnificent buildings are still standing. It
was one of the chief members of the Decapolis, ten cities
that, at the opening of the Christian period, banded together
in a confederacy of Greek-speaking people for mutual defense
and trade propaganda. These cities were all on the great
highroads of Eastern Palestine, only Beth-shean, the ancient
Scythopolis, being to the west. Each city had an outlying
country district. Later more than ten cities were included.
The cultured and wealthy of that part of the world were
gathered in them. Christ visited many of them in this region.
Once so throbbing with life, this section to-day is deserted,
and even the sites of most of its towns are gone. Heaps of
desolate ruins are all that mark ancient sites of a wondrous
civilization. *Ramoth-Gilead* is another of the disputed sites,
the city where Ahab died (1 Kings 22 : 34); the city which
Hazael captured (2 Kings 8 : 28; 9 : 14); the city where
Jehu was proclaimed king (2 Kings 9 : 4. See also Deut.
4 : 43; 1 Kings 4 : 13.) It was also a City of Refuge. That
is was somewhere in this general locality seems, however,
certain. *Mizpah* is supposed to be *Suf,* a village three miles
south of Geresa, where Jacob and Laban erected "a heap of
witnesses," a monument of stone to seal their covenant. (Gen.
31 : 44.) *Rabbath-Ammon,* the ancient capital of the Am-
monites, is on the south side of the Arnon, to the east.
Israel did not purpose to make war on either Ammon or
Moab, since they were descendants of Lot. But they hired
Balaam to come to curse Israel, and Joab. in the time of
David captured Rabbath. In front of its walls, Uriah the
Hittite was slain. (See Deut. 2 : 9, 19; Num. 22; 2 Sam.
11 : 1; 12 : 26.) In New Testament times, this was called
Philadelphia. The ruins of Philadelphia are still extant.
The Land of Moab lies to the east of the Dead Sea, from

the Arnon down about fifteen miles. It is a treeless plateau, 4,300 feet above the Dead Sea. It was held by the Moabites, though they also claimed some land north of the Arnon, during certain periods.

In this land Elimelech and Naomi found refuge and David trusted his aged parents to the king of Moab, although later he waged a bitter war against these people. (See Judg. 11 : 12-18; Ruth 1; 4 : 9; S. Matt. 1 : 5-15; 1 Sam. 22 : 3; 2 Sam. 8 : 2.) Among the cities of Biblical interest we mention *Beth-peor* just east of the head of the Salt Sea, the burial-place of Moses. (Josh. 13 : 20; Deut. 34 : 6.) *Heshbon* lies farther east on the same straight line, on a lofty elevation, 200 feet above the surrounding Plain, fifteen miles east of the Sea. Heshbon was the capital of the Amorite king, Sihon, who captured it from the Moabites. (Num. 21 : 26.) Later it was captured by the Moabites again. (Isa. 15 : 4; Jer. 48 : 34; Josh. 21 : 39.) Six miles south of Heshbon is *Medeba,* before which Joab fought a terrific battle with the combined forces of Syria and Ammon, winning the day for Israel. (1 Chron. 19 : 6.) *Dibon* is on a straight line, 9 or 10 miles south of Medeba. It is mentioned in Num. 21 : 30; 33 : 34; Isa. 15 : 2. Here it was that Dr. Klein discovered the famous Moabite Stone in 1868, a black basalt slab 3½ by 2 feet in size, now in the Louvre at Paris. It records an important account of the oppression of Moab by Omri of Israel and the deliverance under Mesha of Moab. It is dated 900 B. C. The characters are in Phoenician. (See 2 Kings 3 : 3-5.) *Kir of Moab* lies about six miles south of the Arnon. It was a noted Moabite stronghold. (Num. 21 : 28; Isa. 15 : 1; 2 Kings 3 : 26.) Here Mesha was besieged by the forces of Israel and Edom.

Edom or Mt. Seir, called *Idumea* in the New Testament, is the strip of hilly country just south of Moab, lying between the Desert of Arabia and the Wilderness of Paran. *The Brook Zered* separates it from Moab on the north. This Zered was the stream which Israel crossed, under the orders that terminated their long period of wanderings in the wilderness, and began their onward march of conquest into the Promised Land. (See Num. 21 : 12 and Deut. 2 : 13, 14.)

Ancient Edom was 100 miles long and about 20 wide. *Mount Hor* is along its eastern border towards the north. On the top to-day is a Muhammadan temple, erected over the traditional site of Aaron's tomb. (Num. 20 : 23; 33 : 37.) *Bozrah*, the old capital of Edom, lies at the northern portion. *Petra or Selah* is near Mt. Hor. (2 Kings 14 : 7.) It possesses a marvelous rock-hewn Roman temple. When Chedorlaomer swept over Mount Seir or Edom, the country was occupied by the Horites, or mountaineers. (Gen. 14 : 6.) During the Exodus, the Edomites forbade the Israelites passage through their land. (Num. 20 : 14.) They were conquered by David and held subject to his successors. (2 Sam. 8 : 14; 2 Kings 8 : 20; 14 : 1-8; 2 Chron. 25 : 1-14; 28 : 17.) They united with Chaldea against Judah, and were condemned for this action. (Psa. 137 : 7; Ezek. 25 : 12.) Later they were overthrown by the Amalekites from south of the Negeb. The Nabatheans, descendants of Ishmael, then overran the country. Aretas, their king, was father-in-law to Herod Antipas.

Questions and Manual Work on Chapter IX.

1. Take a sheet of paper 8 x 12 inches. Fold three times the short way and four times the long way. Get an outline map of the Eastern World and rule it off the same way as the paper is creased. Transfer by the eye the enlargement to your folded sheet. The Coast Line of the Great Sea falls within the upper squares of the second row. The point of Sinai peninsula falls in the same vertical line. The Euphrates and Tigris rivers lie across the upper and middle third tiers and the middle right tier. Palestine Proper lies entirely within the middle second tier.

2. Locate on this map, which we will call the Eastern Bible World, the places noted in this Chapter.

3. Make a list of the places, their names, events of historical interest, and Bible references.

CHAPTER X

The Plain of Esdraelon

One zone of Palestine yet remains to be explored, the Sixth, as Professor Kent terms it, far up north. It is the PLAIN OF ESDRAELON, and, unlike all the others, it cuts across the Central Plateau from east to west. It is a rough triangle, one angle being at Mount Carmel, one down south in the hills of Samaria, and the third at Mount Tabor and Galilee. It is a huge, level, treeless plain, watered by the muddy Kishon. It has been called the key to Palestine, for its valleys connect in every direction with all the other zones. It has, through all ages, been the great battlefield of the nations. Esdraelon is the Greek word for *Jezreel,* which is translated "God's sowing," a tribute to the extreme fertility of this plain. The main section of the plain is often called the *Valley of Megiddo.* Among the noted battles, the fields of which were almost clearly visible to our blessed Lord when as a youth or man he climbed the hills within a few minutes' walk from his home at Nazareth, scenes that must have stirred his patriotic heart to a tumult are the following:—Deborah's battle with the Canaanites occurred at Mount Tabor when Sisera was slain by the wife of Heber the Kenite (Judg. 5, 6); and Gideon's victory over the Midianites at Mount Gilboa, with the hosts of Midian at *Mt. Moreh.* Here is still Gideon's Spring, where the 300 lapped water, and put to flight Midian and Amalek. (Judg. 6. 7.) On this great battlefield, near Shunem, Saul and Jonathan were slain by the Philistines, who had come up the Maritime Plain and into Esdraelon by way of Megiddo. (1 Sam. 28.) Still again, the saddest defeat Israel ever met, and the one that decided forever her overthrow, was the

death of the promising young king Josiah on the Plain of
Megiddo, as Pharaoh-Necho, the monarch of Egypt, sought
to battle with the king of Babylon. Josiah had been Israel's
hope, a good king and a reformer, and with his death all
her hopes vanished. (2 Kings 23 : 28; 2 Chron. 35 : 20.)
Here Jehu met his doom, as he raged in his chariot up the
Valley of Jezreel, striving against the kings of Israel and
Judah. (2 Kings 9.) The Maccabees, the Romans, the
Arabs, the Crusaders, and Napoleon himself all fought and
struggled on this same sacred ground. The author of Revelation called it Armageddon, in token of its many conflicts.
(Rev. 16 : 16.)

Let us locate some of these most historic places. *Megiddo,*
now known as *Lejjun,* lies about the center of the lower
border of the Plain, in the general direction of the continua-
tion, southeasterly, of the Carmel range of mountains. *Taanach,* mentioned five times in the Bible in connection with
Megiddo, was a stronghold of the Canaanites, situated four
or five miles southeast of Megiddo. Not far from it is
Hadad Rimmon, where the great mourning for Josiah was
held. (Zech. 12 : 11.) Half-way over to the Valley of the
Jordan and a little to the north lies *Jezreel,* the modern
Zerin, now a collection of rude huts, formerly the magnificent
royal residence of Ahab and his evil court. Gideon and
Saul, Elijah and Naboth, Joram, Ahaziah, and Jehu, all had
to do with this city. (1 Kings 21; 2 Kings 9 : 34.) Traveling northeast, we come to *Shunem,* the home of the Shu-
nammite woman whose guest-room was open to Elisha, and
whose son the prophet restored to life. (2 Kings 4.) Abishag
dwelt there, and also the fair woman of Canticles. (1 Kings
1 : 3, 4; Cant. 6 : 13.)

The Valley of Jezreel is the eastern extension of the Plain
of Esdraelon. It is watered chiefly by the *Brook Jalud,*
emptying into the Jordan, and rising in the *Ain Jalud, the
Fountain of Jezreel,* at the foot of Mount Gilboa. This is the
supposed *Fountain or Spring of Gideon.* (Judg. 7.) Here,
too, king Saul camped, just previous to his defeat and death.
(1 Sam. 28 : 4; 29 : 1; 31 : 1.) Far over, southeast, towards
the Jordan Valley, is *Bethshan or Scythopolis,* an old strong-

RUINS OF NEW TESTAMENT
JERICHO

FOUNTAIN OF ELISHA
Photo by S. U. Mitman

RIVER ABANA
Photo by S. U. Mitman

DAMASCUS

DAMASCUS,
Street called Straight

BALBEC RUINS

ANTIOCH IN SYRIA
Photo by W. H. Rau

ANTIOCH OF PISIDIA
Photo by W. H. Rau

hold of the Canaanites, held by them long after the Conquest. (Judg. 1 : 27.) The bodies of Saul and Jonathan were hung on its walls and rescued from there by the men of Jabesh-Gilead. (1 Sam. 31 : 12-13.) There are three mountains of importance in this Plain of Esdraelon, all of them connected with decisive events. From the north downwards, we see *Mount Tabor,* near the foot of the Sea of Tiberias, the most noticeable landmark in lower Galilee. It is not a ridge, but a single mountain, a cone, cut off at the top. From Mount Tabor, the view reaches to the Mediterranean, to Mount Ebal, and to Mount Hermon. Here Barak and Deborah met; here the brothers of Gideon were slain; here some traditions place the Transfiguration of our Lord, though it is unlikely that it occurred at this spot. (Judg. 4 : 5; 8 : 18.) *Little Hermon, or the Hill of Moreh,* is the next mountain, across the valley southward, historic by reason of Gideon's victory (Judg. 7 : 1) and of Saul's witch of Endor. (1 Sam. 28 : 4, 7-25.) The village of *Nain* is on the side of the mountain towards the north, where was restored to life the son of the widow of Nain. (S. Luke 7 : 11.) *Endor* is but two miles northeast of Nain on the same slope of the mountain. In addition to its connection with the witch episode, it was the spot where Barak slew the chiefs of the Canaanites. (Psa. 83 : 10.) The third mountain, still farther south, is *Mount Gilboa,* a ridge or range, about ten miles, from 500 to 1,500 feet high in part. *Jezreel* is on a spur at one end, while *Bethshan* is at the other. On the northern slope Saul and Jonathan met their fate. (2 Sam. 1 : 19.)

Questions and Manual Work on Chapter X.

1. Take an outline map of Esdraelon and mark on it in red ink the sites of all cities, places, mountains, valleys, etc., of which you have learned in this or previous lessons. Put flags for the battlefields.

2. How many and what battlefields were there? What crises did they determine?

3. What places were visited by our Lord?

4. In which ones did He perform miracles and what?

5. Make a paper-pulp map of Esdraelon and color in inks.

CHAPTER XI

THE EASTERN EMPIRES

Far over across *the Arabian Desert,* known as the *Land of Uz or Kedar,* we come to another section of Asia, also a Bible land, which we must hastily explore. From the great highlands of present-day **Armenia,** over 7,000 feet above the sea, there stretches a mighty plain, 700 miles to the Persian Gulf, lying between the great rivers, *the Euphrates* on the west and *the Tigris* on the east. It has been called the *Land of the Twin Rivers.* The upper section was named PADAN ARAM, and later, by the Greeks, *Mesopotamia* or the Land between the Rivers. The lower portion was **Shinar or Caldea.** The northern division is mountainous limestone and gypsum. The lower is low-level land, reclaimed from the ocean below by filling-in from the deposits of earth carried down by the rivers. It is still growing at the rate of over 75 feet a year. The lower plain has not a mineral or stone of any kind. Both the rivers rise, one on either side of *Lake Van,* in Armenia, 150 miles apart. The entire country to-day is a scene of barrenness and desolation, inhabited only by wandering Bedouin Arabs. The cities have disappeared, and only tells, or mounds of earth, mark their sites. These tells are the heaps of ruined walls and houses, all having been made of clay bricks, which in the long years have disintegrated and crumbled away. Beneath these mounds are the lost cities. In 1820 men began to seek out these ancient cities and explore them. From the middle of this past century on, great explorers and men of science and learning have devoted lives and money to the labor of digging out the buried ruins, and rich biblical treasures have amply repaid them.

We will begin with **Caldea,** also called *Shinar* and *Babylonia,* in the south. This is the plain south of *Bagdad.* The

54

early inhabitants were Cushites, of the stock of Ham. *Ur of the Caldees (Mugheir)* was the birthplace of Abram. The first empire began there, probably in 2800 B. C., and lasted till about 538 B. C. Babylon then became the capital. *Borsippa* is the ruins of Birs Nimrud, near Babylon, the supposed situation of the Tower of Babel. The remains of the stage tower seem to have been identified. *Nippur, Nifur,* is on the canal or *River Chebar,* in the central part of the plain south of Babylon. It was the sanctuary of the heathen god, Bel. A wonderful library has been brought to light here, some tablets being as ancient as 2000 B. C.

Above Babylon lies **Mesopotamia,** *Aram-naharaim, the Syria* of the Two Rivers. The northern part contains *Orfa* or *Edessa* and *Haran,* Abram's city of sojourn on the way to Canaan. Mesopotamia is mentioned in the Bible only once as a kingdom (Judg. 3 : 8), for later it was a part of the rising kingdom of Assyria.

The next tier of kingdoms, looking eastward, begins with **Armenia** on the north, a translation of the name Ararat, on some mountain peak of which Noah's Ark rested after the flood. (Gen. 8 : 4.) Next south comes **Assyria,** always *Asshur* in the Bible, now the kingdom of Kurdistan, a mountain range separating it from Armenia on the north. It runs half-way down the Tigris on the south. *Nineveh,* the capital of Assyria under Sennacherib (700 B. C.), is on the east bank of the Tigris, towards the north. Very recently it has been unearthed and explored. The wonderful palace of this king is being uncovered, supposed to have been the most extensive and magnificent in the world. Seventy-one rooms have already been explored. Enormous libraries of clay tablet brick books have been uncovered, all written in cuneiform or wedge-shaped letters on baked clay, containing records of untold value both for history and for the corroboration of the Bible. The famous library of Asshurbanipal is among them. The books are being gradually translated and published. The story of the archæological discoveries in Babylonia, Palestine and Egypt reads like tales of entrancing adventure, and will well repay farther study by the reader. *Calah,* the ruins of *Nimrud,* is 18 miles below Nineveh, on the Tigris. It was an early capital. (Gen. 10 : 11.) It was here that the great Black Obelisk was found. *Dur-sharrukin,* where Sargon's palace was built, covering more than 25 acres, is 18 miles northeast of Nineveh. It is probable that all the four cities noted in Genesis 10 : 11, 12 were within the wall surrounding Nineveh. **Elam or Susiana** lies next south, between *the Zagros Mountains* and the Tigris River. *Susa or Shushan* was its capital, and later on the capital of the Medo-Persian empire. The mound that covers it is partly unearthed. The palace of Esther has been discovered. (Esther 1.) The most important "find" is a cut slab with the law code of Khammurabi, king of Shinar in the time of Abram, many of the laws being closely akin to the laws of Moses in the Bible.

On the east of the *Persian Gulf* lies **Persia,** a small land, and mostly a barren region. *Persipolis,* in the center, one of its ancient capitals, has splendid ruins, showing it to have been a great city once. Persia did not rise into power until Babylon fell, 536 B. C. It then ruled over all lands from India to Ethiopia and became the greatest of all the empires. It was overthrown by Alexander the Great in 330 B. C. Its capital then was Susa, Shushan, of which we have learned.

Still farther east, reaching to the Caspian Sea and beyond, lies **Media,** the old *Madai.* (Gen. 10 : 2.) The Medes were of Aryan or Japhetic descent. The empire of Media arose in 633 B. C., conquered Assyria, Armenia, and Persia, and became the Medo-Persian Empire, overcoming the Babylonian in 536 B. C., afterwards to be swallowed up by Persia. It is part of the kingdom of Persia to-day. The Persians who come to America are from the neighborhood of *Lake Urumiah,* to the east of the Caspian Sea.

Syria, the Hebrew *Aram,* used very indefinitely to include even Palestine, is in its proper sense applied to that region north of Mount Hermon and east of Phœnicia, to the desert on the east and Amanus Mountains on the north. The only point where it touches the Mediterranean is near the mouth of the Orontes. There are three divisions to this land. On the north it is AN ELEVATED PLATEAU, thinly inhabited. Between the *Anti-Lebanon and Lebanon Mountains* is COELE-SYRIA or *Hollow Syria,* with the *Orontes* flowing north in it and the

LYSTRA

TARSUS
Photo by W. H. Rau

MILETUS
Photo by W. H. Rau

EPHESUS
Photo by W. H. Rau

TROAS
Photo by Riley

PHILIPPI
Photo by W. H. Rau

ATHENS
General View
Photo by S. U. Mitman

ATHENS, MARS HILL
Photo by S. U. Mitman

Litany flowing south. The third section is the eastern level
PLAIN OF DAMASCUS, of which we have spoken in dealing
with the zone of Palestine, east of the Jordan. Among the
important cities not treated before is *Carchemish*, on the upper Euphrates, the ruins of which are found at Jerablus
now. It was for centuries the capital of the ancient Hittite
kingdom. Another is *Antioch in Syria*, not to be confounded
with the other Antioch in Pisidia (Asia Minor). S. Paul
visited both of these towns.

It was captured by Pharaoh-Necho after the victory at
Megiddo (608 B. C.), but Nebuchadnezzar retook it three
years later. (2 Chron. 35 : 20; Jer. 46 : 2.) *Hamath* is on
the Orontes, near the northern limits of Palestine. Its king
sent presents to David when he defeated the king of Zobah.
It is mentioned frequently in the Bible. (Look up Num.
13 : 21 ; 34 : 8; 2 Sam. 8 : 8; 2 Chron. 8 : 4; 2 Kings 14 : 28;
18 : 14; 19 : 13.) *Tadmor or Palmyra,* the City of Palms,
is in an oasis about 150 miles from Damascus, northeast.
It is mentioned, too, in the Bible and has now extensive
ruins remaining. (2 Chron. 8 : 4; 1 Kings 9 : 18.) *Baalbec,* See opp. p. 53
the *City of Baal* or *City of the Sun,* the Greek *Heliopolis,* is
in Coele-Syria, 35 miles from Damascus. There are wonderful ruins there to-day, two great temples and other buildings,
often visited by travelers. *Riblah* is on the Orontes, 35 miles
from Baalbec. Pharaoh-Necho and Nebuchadnezzar both had
headquarters there. *Antioch, in Syria,* was founded about See opp. p. 53
300 B. C., and is located towards the mouth of the Orontes.
It was the capital of Syria for a long period, and the third
most important city in the Roman empire, coming next to
Rome and Alexandria. It was here that the disciples were
first called Christians. It was named Antioch the Beautiful
and the Crown of the East. It is now a city of some 6,000
souls. *Seleucia,* at the mouth of this same river, was the Port
of Antioch.

Questions and Manual Work on Chapter XI.

1. On your creased-paper outline map of the Eastern World,
color in in crayons or water colors the kingdoms mentioned
in this chapter.

2. Mark in and name the cities and places.

3. See the Historical Old Testament Maps in the Appendix and note which kingdoms in order rose into power and waned.

CHAPTER XII

Asia Minor is the peninsula at the northwest corner of the
Continent of Asia, jutting out towards Greece between the
Mediterranean and the Black (Euxine) Seas. It was com-
posed of some fourteen provinces (ten of which are men-
tioned in the New Testament), combined under the Roman
government, politically, into seven. On the north *Bithynia*
(Acts 16 : 7; 1 S. Peter 1 : 1), *Paphlagonia, and Pontus*
(Acts 2 : 9; 18 : 2; 1 S. Peter 1 : 1) formed the Roman
PROVINCE OF BITHYNIA AND PONTUS. To the west, *Mysia*
(Acts 16 : 7, 8), *Lydia, Caria* and part of *Phrygia* formed the
PROVINCE OF ASIA. When Asia is mentioned in the Bible it
never means the Continent, but this Province. Southeast of
Asia is *Lycia* (Acts 27 : 5) ; next comes *Pamphylia.* (Acts
13 : 13.) Then *the Kingdom of Antiochus,* then *Cilicia.*
(Acts 6 : 9.) North of the Kingdom of Antiochus was *Cap-
padocia* (Acts 2 : 9), and in the very center was the large
Province of *Galatia,* including Lycaonia. (Acts 14 : 1-23.)
Excepting Jews and Jewish converts, all the inhabitants of
this vast region of 156,000 square miles were idolaters, with
many gods and many religions. Most of the people were
Greek colonists ; some were Romans, some Jews, and many
native races. These latter lived chiefly outside of the large
cities, which were occupied by Greeks, Romans, and Jews.

Looking at each province in order, we find that S. Paul did
not enter BITHYNIA-PONTUS at all, though S. Peter in his
First Epistle sends a greeting to Christians of Bithynia and
of Pontus. He also does likewise for the Christians of
CAPPADOCIA, some of whom heard him on the Day of Pente-
cost at Jerusalem. (Acts 1.) S. Paul did not visit this

province either. GALATIA, as a province, included *Galatia* proper, a region settled by Gauls about 300 B. C., and *South Galatia,* composed of *Lycaonia, Pisidia,* and part of *Phrygia. Ancyra* was the capital of the whole province. It is now called *Angora,* and was the source of the Angora goats.

See opp. p. 53 *Antioch* was the principal city of South Galatia, to be carefully distinguished from Antioch in Syria. This one was called Antioch towards Pisidia, though it was actually in Phrygia. S. Paul visited it, and found a goodly Jewish colony settled there. (Acts 13 : 14.)

Iconium, Lystra, and Derbe are other important cities, all of them visited by S. Paul in his several missionary journeys.

See opp. p. 56 It was at *Lystra* that the citizens thought S. Paul and S. Barnabas were gods and tried to worship them. The uncertainty of the use of the name "Galatia," whether intending to designate simply the northern portion of the Province or the whole of it, has given rise to the controversy as to the Epistle to the Galatians, written by S. Paul. The general view to-day, called the South Galatian View, is that it was intended for the Christians of *Lystra, Derbe, Iconium, and Antioch,* and that S. Paul never visited the northern district

See opp. p. 56 at all. In CILICIA, *Tarsus* was the principal city, and was famous for being the birthplace of S. Paul. In LYCIA, *Myra,* the capital, was three miles from the mouth of a river. S. Paul stopped there on the last voyage to Rome. (Acts 27 : 5.) *Patara* was near the mouth of the *River Xanthus,* an important commercial city, devoted to the worship of Apollo. (Acts 21 : 1.) S. Paul also stopped there. ASIA was the largest of the Provinces of Asia Minor, and the most im-

See opp. p. 56 portant. In the subdivision, Caria, was the town of *Miletus,* one of the leading Ionian cities. Messengers were sent to this town by S. Paul. (Acts 20 : 15-17.) In the Lydia sub-

See opp. p. 56 division is *Ephesus,* the capital of the province, and the greatest trade center of that region, owing to its fine harbor. Here was centered the worship of Diana, the Roman equivalent of the Greek Artemis. A rich business in making silver shrines of the goddess was carried on in this town. (Acts 19 : 24.) S. Paul spent much time and wrought great results here. Smyrna, forty miles from Ephesus, had as its chief

CORINTH, OLD
Photo by W. H. Rau

CORINTH, MODERN
Photo by Williams, Brown & Earle

CENCHREA
Photo by W. H. Rau

MITYLENE
Photo by W. H. Rau

ISLAND OF PATMOS
Photo by Williams, Brown & Earle

MALTA
Photo by Williams, Brown & Earle

SYRACUSE
Photo by W. H. Rau

RHEGIUM
Photo by Williams, Brown & Earle

gods, Nemesis and Dionysus, the god of wine. Ignatius, the Christian Bishop of Smyrna, was thrown to wild beasts and met his death as a martyr in the amphitheater here, and here also Bishop Polycarp, a disciple of S. John, was burned at the stake. *Sardis, Philadelphia,* and *Thyatira* are other cities of this same district, the former noted for its dyers' guilds (Acts 16 : 14) and both mentioned in the letters to the Seven Churches in Revelation, Chapters 2 and 3.

In the Phrygia district are *Laodicaea* and *Colosse,* cities which S. Paul does not seem to have visited; but which are mentioned in his writings. (See Acts 20 : 17; 21 : 1; Col. 4 : 9, 12, 16, 17.) They may have been founded by S. Paul's helpers, while he was laboring at Ephesus. *Colosse* was the home of Philemon, Onesimus, and Epaphros. *Pergamos,* in MYSIA, is said, at one time, to have been the most beautiful city in all Asia Minor. It had a magnificent temple to Aphrodite and another to Esculapius. *Troas* was another See opp. p. 57 important city of the same district, situated on the Aegean Sea.

We now cross over to **Greece.** All the places visited by S. Paul and his co-workers in this section are included in Achaia and **Macedonia,** provinces of the Roman Empire. ACHAIA was the Roman name for the little land of Greece, the ruling state of which was Achaia, from which the name was applied to the whole region. MACEDONIA was the district north of Achaia, famous for its mighty kings, Philip of Macedon and Alexander the Great. Crossing from Troas, in Mysia, S. Paul went first to *Philippi* (Acts 16 : 12-40), See opp. p. 57 named after Philip, the father of Alexander. Near it was fought the world-battle between Augustus and Antony, and Brutus and Cassius, which crushed the hope of a Roman republic and began the empire. It was a Roman colony and its rulers bore Roman titles. Here Lydia the first European convert was baptized, a church was founded, S. Paul and Silas were scourged, a jailer was converted to Christianity, and much people brought to the Master. (See Acts 16 : 3, 9-12; 1 Thess. 1 : 7, 8.) It was called the Chief City of Macedonia in the Book of Acts. *Neapolis* was the port of Philippi. *Amphipolis* was 33 miles southwest of Philippi, three miles from the sea. In S. Paul's time, it had started on the wane, having no synagogue and few, if any, Jews. He tarried there but a day. (Acts 17 : 1.) *Thessalonica* was the capital of the whole province. It was forty miles from Amphipolis. It had a synagogue and many Jews dwelt there. S. Paul founded there a Church of Gentiles, and wrote two Epistles to them. The people stirred up a riot and expelled the Apostles from the city. At the present day, under the name *Saloniki,* it ranks as the second city of European Turkey, with a population of 80,000 persons. (See Acts 17 : 1-9; 1 Thess. 1 : 7, 8.) *Berea* (Acts 17 : 10-13), thirty-five miles from the preceding, was a small city, selected by S. Paul because of its retirement. Its inhabitants accepted the Gospel gladly, giving eager attention to its preachment. In fact the title Berean has stood as a synonym for faithful Bible students ever since.

See opp. p. 57 In ACHAIA OR GREECE, *Athens* was the most famous city of all the world. (Acts 17 : 15-34.) It was situated on a jutting promontory on the south, surrounded by noted mountains, and See opp. p. 57 itself cut up in the center by four hills; the Acropolis, surmounted by the Parthenon; the Areopagus, where S. Paul preached his startling sermon; the Pnyx; and the Museum. In S. Paul's time, Athens, though not the political center, was still the literary focus of the Empire. No church appears to have been founded by S. Paul, as the outcome of this sermon; but four centuries later, that very Parthenon became a Christian church and the Athenians the most hostile foes of image worship. It had been the chief city of images and shrines before. All the gods were honored, Apollo, Zeus, Bacchus, Mercury, etc., all had temples. On Mars' Hill, the Areopagus met, the famous Council or Court, from which the hill was named. In the Parthenon, the temple of Pallas, was the great statue of ivory and gold made by Phidias.

See opp. p. 60 *Corinth* was at the middle of the Grecian Isthmus, with two Ports, east and west, *Cenchreae* and *Lechaeum.* (Acts See opp. p. 60 18 : 1-18.) It was forty miles from Athens. *The Isthmus* is here 10 miles wide. It was the residence of the Proconsul and the commercial and political center of Greece. A very wicked and licentious city it was, and near it were celebrated the Isthmian games. S. Paul preached in Corinth a year and a half, working at his trade of tent-making. Here he wrote the two Epistles to the Thessalonians. After he left Corinth, he addressed the Corinthians two Epistles. During the wars with Rome, Corinth was utterly sacked and destroyed. For a century it lay in ruins. Then it was rebuilt and became a Roman colony. Now only a tiny village marks its desolate site. *Cenchreae* (Acts 18 : 18) was the city where S. Paul See opp. p. 60 cut off his hair in the Levitical vow and established a Church (Rom. 16 : 1, 2) and had a deaconess there, named Phebe.

There are several Islands of importance in Bible history.
Some are in the AEGEAN SEA and some in the MEDITERRANEAN. In the AEGEAN SEA, we have, beginning at the northern end, *Samothracia,* a small but lofty island; *Mitylene or Lesbos,* See opp. p. 60 famous as the home of the Greek poetess, Sappho (Acts 26 : 14) ; *Chios,* another island, said to have been the birthplace of Homer (Acts 20 : 15) ; *Samos,* the birthplace of Pythagoras, the philosopher (Acts 20 : 15) ; *Patmos,* twenty See opp. p. 6 miles south of Samos, was the island of S. John's apocalyptic vision recorded in the Book of Revelation. *Trogyllium,* a town or cape on Asia Minor, the anchorage of S. Paul's party, still called *"S. Paul's Port"* (Acts 20 : 15) ; *Coos,* now called *Stanchio* (Acts 21 : 1) and, in the MEDITERRANEAN, *Rhodes,* an island of note, 46 miles long and 18 miles wide, where the figure of Colossus stood, 100 feet high, overthrown by an earthquake and so prostrate at S. Paul's visit (Acts 21 : 1) ; *Cyprus,* named from its rich copper mines (Greek, Kupros, copper), spoken of in the Old Testament as Chittim (Isa. 23 : 12), whose favorite goddess was Aphrodite, the birthplace of S. Barnabas, governed when S. Paul passed it (Acts 27 : 4) by a proconsul, ruling over four large cities, *Paphos, Salamis, Amathus,* and *Citium; Crete or Candia,* at the entrance of the Aegean Sea, an island with an area of 3,300 square miles, with 100 cities to its credit (Acts 2 : 11), among which was *Fair Havens,* where S. Paul's vessel touched for anchorage and temporary safety (Acts 27 : 7-13), (over this island, S. Titus ruled as Bishop (Titus 1 : 5) a little later; *Malta,* the ancient *Melita,* now under British rule, on which See opp. p. 61 island the vessel was shipwrecked (Acts 28 : 7) and where

the prisoners stayed all winter, setting sail for Rome in the spring.

Italy is our only remaining, untraversed Bible land.
At its foot was the great island of SICILY. On the last Voyage
See opp. p. 61 to Rome, S. Paul stopped at *Syracuse,* on the eastern shore.
See opp. p. 61 (Acts 28 : 12.) The next important town is *Rhegium,* at
the toe of the Italian boot, now the flourishing town of
Rheggio. (Acts 28 : 13.) Half-way up the Italian coast
towards Rome is *Puteoli,* near Naples, one of the lead-
ing ports of Italy, being to Rome what Liverpool is to Lon-
don. Here S. Paul found a Christian Church and remained
See opp. p. 64 a week. The city is now *Pozzuoli.* At a place, called *Appii*
See opp. p. 64 *Forum,* the Forum of Appius, *the Appian Way,* 43 miles from
Rome, and again at *Three Taverns,* 10 miles on, S. Paul
stopped, met Christians, and received a welcome. (Acts
See opp. p. 64 28 : 15.) *Rome* stands on the river Tiber. In its glory it
spread over ten hills, though tradition says it was founded
on seven. Here S. Paul remained in prison. Here some
See opp. p. 64 years later, he and S. Peter suffered martyrdom. S. Paul
was imprisoned in his own hired house near the Pretorian
Camp, while the Jewish Quarter was on the opposite side of
the City. At this time, Rome had about 1,200,000 inhabitants,
one-half of whom were slaves, and two-thirds of the rest
paupers, supported by free food from the rich. In Rome,
S. Paul wrote the Epistles to the Ephesians, Colossians,
Philippians, and Philemon. After two years he was released,
and probably spent two years or more in preaching before his
final imprisonment and death.

Questions and Manual Work on Chapter XII.

1. Draw a map of Asia Minor giving every Province and
District, i.e. noting those absorbed by the Roman Empire into
a few provinces.

2. Locate the cities visited by S. Paul and the events noted
at each.

3. Locate the remaining cities of importance not visited
by S. Paul, using a different color for marking.

4. Draw a separate map of Greece and locate the cities and
events.

POZZUOLI
Photo by W. H. Rau

APPIAN WAY
Photo by W. H. Rau

PALACE OF THE CAESARS
Rome

COLISEUM
Copyrighted by Underwood & Underwood

5. Take a Map of the Roman World and locate all the islands, and make mention of events.

6. Do the same with Italy.

7. Take four such maps and from the key maps in the Appendix reproduce each of S. Paul's four journeys.

THE WORLD ON MERCATOR PROJECTION
Showing position and size of Palestine

PHYSICAL MAP OF PALESTINE.

WESTERN ASIA
(EARLY TIMES)

Caspian Sea

MEDIA

ELAM

CHALDEA

Mt. Ararat
17,000 ft.

ASSYRIA

Babel
R. Tigris
Calnah
Shinar
Accad
Ur of Chaldees
(Mugheir)

BABYLONIA

Nineveh
Resen Calah

Mesopotamia

R. Euphrates

Haran
(Padan Aram?)

Arabian Desert

Damascus

S Y R I A

Hamath

Sidon

CANAAN

Shechem
Beth-el
Hebron
Beer-sheba

KITTIM

THE   GREAT

SEA

EGYPT
OR
MIZRAIM

SINAI

Persian Gulf

0   50   100   150   200   250

THE PERIOD
OF THE
PATRIARCHS

SCALE OF MILES

0   100   200   300   400

Abraham's Route ——

THE PERIOD
OF THE EXODUS

PERIOD OF THE
TRIBAL
SETTLEMENTS

SCALE OF MILES

0   10   20   30   40   50

ASSYRIANS

HITTITES

THE GREAT SEA

Tripolis

MT. NOR

Rehob

Sidon

MT. HERMON
Abanah
Damascus
R. Pharpar

Tyre
Achzib Ramah
Accho
Ptolemais

Waters of
Meron

Dan

Sea of
Chinnereth
Aphek

HILLS OF

MT. CARMEL
Dor

Jabesh
Endor

BASHAN

Edrei

Dothan Tirzah
Samaria
Shechem
Adam

Jabesh-Gilead
Ramath-Gilead

Joppa

Shiloh
Gibeon Jericho
Bethel

Penuel
AMMONITES

Kirjath-Jearim
JERUSALEM
Nob

Gath
Socoh Bethlehem
Ekron Hebron
Eshcol

Beth-Peor
H. Heshbon
MT. NEBO

Askelon

Gaza

Brook Besor
Gerar
Beer-Sheba

Ziklag
Etam
Ziph

R. Arnon

Aroer

THE NEGEB

MT. HOR

DESERT TRIBES

Engedi

Salt
Sea
Ar
Kir

MOABITES

Wilderness
of Shur

Wilderness
of Zin

Wilderness of Paran

Ezion-geber

Elath

Red
Sea

EDOMITES

AMALEKITES

Hamath

Tadmor

R. Euphrates

Great   Syrian

Desert

PHOENICIANS

LEBANON

Orontes

HERMAEANS

THE PERIOD OF
THE JUDGES
1270-1030

SCALE OF MILES
0   20   40   60   80   100

THE KINGDOM
OF SAUL
1030–1010

SCALE OF MILES

0   20   40   60   80   100

ASSYRIANS

HITTITES

R. Orontes

Hamath

Tadmor

R. Euphrates

Great Syrian

Desert

Tripolis

MT. HOR

Rehob

Sidon

MT. HERMON

R. Abanah

Damascus

Ijon

Dan

R. Pharpar

Tyre

Ramah

Waters of

Merom

Achzib

Accho

Ptolemais

Sea of

Chinnereth

HILLS OF

Aphek

BASHAN

MT. CARMEL

Haberath

Endor

Shunem

R. Hieromax

Edrei

Dor

Jabesh Gilead

Dothan

Tirzah

Ramoth Gilead

Shechem

Succoth

AMMONITES

Joppa

Adam

Shiloh

Penuel

Jericho

Beth Peor

Kirjath Jearim

JERUSALEM

Gibeon

Nob

Heshbon

MT. NEBO

Askelon

Gibeah

Bethlehem

Gaza

Socoh

Hebron

R. Arnon

Aroer

Brook Besor

Eglon

Ziph

Ar

Juttah

Salt

Sea

Beer-Sheba

En Gedi

THE NEGEB

MT. HOR

DESERT TRIBES

Wilderness

Wilderness

of Shur

of Zin

Wilderness of Paran

Ezion-geber

Elath

Red

Sea

THE GREAT SEA

PHOENICIANS

LEBANON

ARAMAEANS

MOABITES

EDOMITES

THE EMPIRE OF
DAVID AND SOLOMON
1000-937

SCALE OF MILES
0   20   40   60   80   100

ASSYRIANS

HITTITES

THE GREAT SEA

Euphrates

R.

Orontes

Hamath

Tadmor

Tripolis

Great Syrian

Desert

Rehob

Sidon

MT.HERMON
Abanah
Damascus
R. Pharpar

Tyre
Achzib
Accho
Ptolemais

Dan
Waters of
Merom
Hazor

Sea of
Chinnereth
Aphek

HILLS OF

BASHAN

MT.CARMEL
Dor

Haberath
Endor
Shunem

Edrei

Dothan
Tirzah
Samaria
Shechem
MT.EBAL

Jabesh-Gilead
Ramoth-Gilead

Joppa
Shiloh
Adam

Penuel

AMMONITES

Jericho

SYRIANS

ISRAEL

PHOENICIA

Kirjath-jearim
Askelon
Gaza
Brook Besor
Gerar
Ziklag
Sheba
Juttah
Engedi

JERUSALEM
Gibeah
Nob
Eshcol
Etam
Ziph

Bethlehem
Hebron

MT.NEBO
Areah
Ar
Kir

Beth-hor

Salt
Sea

MOABITES

THE NEGEB

DOMINIONS

OF

JUDAH

MT.HOR

Wilderness
of Shur

Wilderness
of Zin

Wilderness of Paran

Egypt

Ezion-geber
Elath

Red
Sea

THE
DIVIDED KINGDOM
TO THE
REVOLUTION OF JEHU
937-842

SCALE OF MILES

0   20   40   60   80   100

THE
SYRIAN CONQUESTS
IN THE
REIGN OF HAZAEL
About 814 to 797

SCALE OF MILES
0   20   40   60   80   100

DOMINIONS

R. Orontes

R. Euphrates

OF ASSYRIA

Hamath

Tadmor

Tripolis

MT. HOR

THE GREAT SEA

Rehob

Sidon

MT. HERMON

R. Abana

Damascus

Great Syrian

Tyre

Luz

R. Pharpar

Dan

Desert

Achzib

Ramah

Waters of Merom

Accho

Hazor

Ptolemais

Sea of

Chinnereth

Daberath

Aphek

HILLS OF

MT. CARMEL

Endor

BASHAN

Dor

Shunem

R. Jarmuk

Dothan

Tirzah

Jabesh-Gilead

Edrei

Samaria

Shechem

MT.

EBAL

Ramoth-Gilead

Adam

Joppa

Shiloh

Penuel

AMMONITES

Lydda

Succoth

Jericho

Beth-Peor

SALEM

Nob

Bethel

Heshbon

Kirjath-Jearim

Askelon

Succoh

Bethlehem

MT. NEBO

Gaza

Eshcol

Hebron

Arnon

Brook Besor

Etam

Aroer

Ziph

Beer-sheba

Zephath

Juttah

Salt

Ar

Adar

Engedi

Sea

Kir

THE NEGEB

MT. HOR

Wilderness

of Shur

Wilderness

of Zin

THE ASSYRIAN
CONQUEST OF SYRIA
797–783

Wilderness of Paran

SCALE OF MILES

0   20   40   60   80   100

Ezion-geber

Elath

Red

Sea

THE PERIOD
OF JEROBOAM II
780-740

SCALE OF MILES
0   20   40   60   80   100

THE
CONQUESTS OF
TIGLATH-PILESER III
733-727

SCALE OF MILES
0   20   40   60   80   100

THE
FALL OF ISRAEL
AND THE
PERIOD OF HEZEKIAH
721: 727-695

SCALE OF MILES
0   20   40   60   80   100

THE
SCYTHIAN INVASION
AND THE
PERIOD OF JOSIAH
628: 639-608

SCALE OF MILES
0   20   40   60   80   100

THE
BABYLONIAN PERIOD
605-586

SCALE OF MILES

0   20   40   60   80   100

THE PERIOD
OF THE EXILES
586-536

SCALE OF MILES

0   100   200   300   400

Israel's Captivity
Judah's

THE
PERSIAN PERIOD
536-332

SCALE OF MILES

0   20   40   60   80   100

PALESTINE
IN THE
TIME OF CHRIST

Scale of English Miles.
0   10   20   30   40

SIDON

SYRIA

SAREPTA

DAMASCUS

Pharpar R.

LEBANON MTS.

TYRE
LEONTES

ABILENE

MT. HERMON

CÆSAREA PHILIPPI

PHŒNICIA

ITUREA

GAULANITIS

KADESH

L. HULEH

HAZOR (MEROM)

PTOLEMAIS

ZEBULON

CHORAZIN

BETHSAIDA JULIAS

CAPERNAUM

BETHSAIDA

GALILEE

MAGDALA

SEA OF GALILEE

GERESA?

DECAPOLIS

AURANITIS

CANATHA

SEPPHORIS

TIBERIAS

CANA

NAZARETH

MT. CARMEL

R. Kishon

NAIN

MT. TABOR

ABILA

GADARA

TRACHONITIS

BATANEA

DORA

BETHABARA?

ARBELA

BOZRAH

CÆSAREA

GINEA

SCYTHOPOLIS

PELLA

PLAIN OF SHARON

SAMARIA

SAMARIA

ÆNON

SYCHAR

SHECHEM

SALIM

GERASA

ACRABI

Jabbok R.

MEDITERRANEAN SEA

ANTIPATRIS

SHILOH

ZERKA

EPHRAIM

JOPPA

PHASAELIS

PEREA

PHILADELPHIA

LYDDA

MODIN

BETHEL

M. QUARANTANIA

JAMNIA

NICOPOLIS

EMMAUS?

ADASA

JERICHO

BETHABARA?

AZOTUS

JUDEA

JERUSALEM

BETHANY

HESHBON

ASCALON

BETHLEHEM

HERODIUM

Brook Kidron

THE

BETHSURA

WILDERNESS OF JUDEA

DEAD

MACHÆRUS

GAZA

HEBRON

ENGEDI

SEA

Arnon R.

GERAR

JUTTA

GERARITICA

BEERSHEBA

IDUMEA

MASADA

ARABIA

Brook Zered

HEZRON

Acrabbatene

THE EASTERN PART OF THE
ROMAN EMPIRE
IN THE TIME OF
ST. PAUL

EXPLANATIONS
Names of Roman Provinces in CAPITALS
Local Geographical Names in ITALICS
Boundaries of Provinces ——————

THE PROVINCES
OF
SYRIA AND PALESTINE

0   25   50   75
SCALE OF MILES

THE PROVINCES
OF
SYRIA AND PALESTINE

0   25   50   75
SCALE OF MILES

THE PROVINCES
OF
SYRIA AND PALESTINE

0   25   50   75
SCALE OF MILES

THE PROVINCES
OF
SYRIA AND PALESTINE

0   25   50   75
SCALE OF MILES

THE PROVINCES

OF

SYRIA AND PALESTINE

0   25   50   75
SCALE OF MILES

THE
EARLY CHRISTIAN WORLD

MILES

0   50   100   200   250

THE
EARLY CHRISTIAN WORLD

MILES
0 50 100 200 250

THE
EARLY CHRISTIAN WORLD

MILES

0   50   100   200   250

THE
EARLY CHRISTIAN WORLD

MILES
0   50 100   200 250

THE JOURNEYS OF S. PAUL.

PALESTINE
SHOWING THE
PRINCIPAL ROADS
IN THE
TIME OF CHRIST

Sidon

S Y R I A

Damascus

P H O E N I C I A

Tyre   Cæsarea Philippi

GALILEE   DECAPOLIS

Ptolemais

Capernaum

Sea of Galilee

MEDITERRANEAN SEA

Nazareth

Cæsarea

S A M A R I A

P E R E A

Samaria

Jordan R.

Joppa

Jericho

Jerusalem

A R A B I A

Bethlehem

J U D E A

Hebron

Gaza

The Dead Sea

SCALE OF MILES
0   5   10   20   30   40

Beersheba

ANCIENT

JERUSALEM

Scale of One Roman Mile

JERUSALEM
in the days of
NEHEMIAH
and at the time of the
GOSPELS.

SCALE OF ENGLISH FEET

0   500   1000   1500   2000   2500

Jeremiah's
Grotto
Calvary †

Pool of Bethesda

Damascus Gate

BEZETHA

QUARTER

Hananeel
Tower?   Antonia
Meah Tower?   St. Stephen's
Gate

CHRISTIAN QUARTER   Herod's Zion Temple
sheep Gate

Via Dolorosa   Golden
Gate

Church   Antonia   Gethsemane
of the   Sanhedrin
Holy Sepulchre   Hall   Temple   Solomon's Porch

Mosque of Omar

David Street   Robinson's
Arch?   Water Gate

Jaffa Gate   Palace
of
Herod   JEWISH QUARTER   Mills

Water Gate

Garden   Herod   Gihon

House of Caiaphas

Traditional
Tomb of David   Siloam

Dung Gate

PROBABLE LINE OF NEHEMIAH'S NIGHT RIDE

MOHAMEDAN QUARTER

ARMENIAN QUARTER

MOUNT OF OLIVES

INDEX

A.

Abana, 44.
Abel Meholah, 40.
Abel Shittim, 42.
Abila, 44.
Aceldama, 22.
Adam, 40.
Admah, 41.
Adullam, Cave, 8.
Aelia Capitolina, 25.
Ai, 19.
Aijalon, Valley, 8.
Ain Gadis, 32.
Ain Jalud, 52.
Ain Jidy, 24.
Ain Quadis, 32.
Akabah, 61.
Alexandria, 3.
Amathus, 63.
Amphipolis, 61.
Anathoth, 21.
Ancyra, 60.
Angora, 60.
Anti-Lebanon Mountains, 6, 44, 56.
Antioch in Pisidia, 60.
Antioch in Syria, 57.
Appian Way, 64.
Appii Forum, 64.
Arabah, xiv.
Arabian Desert, 1, 54.
Aram, 56.
Aram-naharaim, 55.
Argob, 46.
Ariel, 25.
Armenian Convent, 25.
Ashdod, 7.
Ashkelon, 7.
Asia Minor, 1, 5.
Asshur, 55.
Athens, 62.
Awaji, 44.

B.

Baalbec, 57.
Baal-Hazor, 15.
Baal-Zephon, 4.
Babylon, 54.
Bagdad, 54.
Banias, 34.
Barada, 44.
Beersheba, 8, 32.
Beitin, 19.
Berea, 62.
Besor, Brook, 8.

Bethany, 24.
Bethel, 12, 19.
Bethesda, 26.
Beth-horon, 32.
Bethlehem, 31.
Beth-peor, 49.
Bethphage, 24.
Bethsaida Julias, 37.
Bethsaida of Galilee, 37.
Beth-Shan, 40, 52, 53.
Beth-Shemesh, 8.
Bithynia, 59.
Black Sea, 1.
Blue Nile, 3.
Books, ix.
Borsippa, 55.
Bozrah, 50.
Brook Besor, 8.
Brook Cherith, 23.
Brook Jabbok, 46.
Brook Jalud, 52.
Brook Zered, 49.

C.

Cæsarea, 7.
Cæsarea Philippi, 6, 34.
Calah, 55.
Calvary, 29.
Cana, xv, 10.
Canaan, 2.
Candia, 63.
Capernaum, 10. 37.
Cappadocia, 59.
Carchemish, 57.
Caria, 59.
Carmel, 6, 13.
Caspian Sea, 1.
Cave Adullam, 8.
Cenchreæ, 62, 63.
Central Mountain Range, 1.
Chebar, 55.
Cherith, Brook, 23.
Chinnereth, Lake, 34.
Chios, 63.
Chorazin, 37.
Church of the Holy Sepulchre, 26.
Church of St. Anne, 26.
Church of St. James, 26.
Cilicia, 59.
Citium, 63.
City of Palm Trees, 40.
Coele Syria, 56.
Colosse, 61.
Coos, 63.

Index

Index

Index

Index

Riblah, 57.
River Tigris, 1, 5, 54.
River Xanthus, 60.
River Yarmuk, 39.
Robinson's Arch, 28.
Rock Rimmon, 19.
Roman Empire, 1.
Rome, 64.
Royal Quarries, 27.

S.

Salamis, 63.
Salem, 25.
Saloniki, 62.
Samaria, Hill of, 15.
Samaria, Modern, 13.
Samaria, N. T., 12.
Samaria, O. T., 12.
Samaria, Pool of, 16.
Samos, 63.
Samothracia, 63.
Sardis, 61.
Scythopolis, 52.
Sea of Galilee, 36.
Sebaste, 16.
Seilun, 16.
Seir, 49.
Selah, 50.
Seleucia, 57.
Sharon, 7.
Shechem, 13.
Shephelah, 8.
Shiloh, 16.
Shinar, 54.
Shunem, 10, 52.
Shur, 3.
Shushan, 56.
Sidon, 6.
Siloam, 29.
Sin, 3.
Sinai, 3.
Sinai Peninsula, 1, 3.
Six Zones, 5.
Slides, xxi.
Sodom, 41.
Sorek, 8.
Southern Desert, 2.
Southen Egypt, 3.
Southern Road, 30.
South Galatia, 60.
Southwestern Road, 31.
Spring of Gideon, 52.
Stanchio, 63.
St. Paul's Port, 63.
St. Stephen's Gate, 26.
Stereopticon Slides, xxi.
Succoth, 4, 40.
Suez, 1.
Suf, 48.
Supplies, ix.
Susa, 56.
Sychar, 14.
Syracuse, 64.
Syria, 1, 55.

T.

Taanach, 52.
Tabor, 9, 53.
Tadnor, 57.
Tarsus, 60.
Tekoa, 24.
Thebes, 3.
The Holy City, 25.
The Holy Land, 2.
Thessalonica, 62.
Three Taverns, 64.
Threshing Floor of Araunah, 28.
Thyatira, 61.
Tiberias, 34, 36.
Tigris, 1, 5, 54.
Timnath, 8.
Tirzah, 15.
Tophet, 22, 29.
Trachonitis, 46.
Troas, 61.
Trogyllium, 63.
Twin Rivers, 54.
Tyre, xxi, 6.
Tyropoeon, 25.

U.

Um-Keis, 47.
Upper Egypt, 3.
Upper Gihon, 29.
Ur of Chaldees, 55.
Urumiah, 56.
Uz, 46, 54.

V.

Vale of Hebron, 31.
Valley of Aijalon, 8.
Valley of Dothan, 13.
Valley of Elah, 8, 31.
Valley of Gihon, 25.
Valley of Hinnom, 22, 25.
Valley of Jehoshaphat, 22, 25.
Valley of Jezreel, 52.
Valley of the Jordan, 39.
Valley of Megiddo, 51.
Valley of Shechem, 13.
Valley of the Sorek, 8.
Van, 54.
Via Dolorosa, 26.
Village of Siloam, 29.

W.

Wailing Place of the Jews, 28.
Watch-tower, 37.
Waters of Merom, 34, 35.
Western Road, 31.
White Nile, 3.
Wilderness of Judah, 23.
Wilderness of Mount Sinai, 3.
Wilderness of Paran, 3.
Wilderness of Shur, 3.
Wilderness of Sin, 3.
Wilderness of Zin, 3.
Wood of Ephraim, 47.

Index